D1213297

PRAISE FOR *EMBRACING PROGRESS*

"Sophie Wade tackles the Future of Work with a compelling big-picture vision and a smart understanding of its details. Her path of learning, questioning, and refining ideas delivers real-world approaches employers can use to help employees perform at their best. Whether dealing with the emerging understanding of creativity, the power of purpose, or the relationship between individuals and groups, Sophie understands the desire for fully coherent workplaces that best empower the workforce of today and tomorrow."

—GREG PARSONS, SENIOR VICE PRESIDENT AND CREATIVE DIRECTOR, WORK AT HERMAN MILLER, INC.

"Sophie Wade has been deeply immersed in the Future of Work for several years, starting with her focus on workplace flexibility. She shares many brilliant insights about the changing demands of the workforce and explains how the workplace is being radically altered forever. Her approach is organic, continually absorbing and developing new perspectives that illuminate the evolution of the Future of Work. The applications are so helpful, supporting companies' adaptions to this very new way of working. You can't go forward without it!"

—FAITH POPCORN, CEO, FAITH POPCORN'S BRAINRESERVE

"Sophie Wade is a prime example that the most imaginative and insightful ideas come from those few among us comfortable traversing traditionally siloed fields and cross-pollinating great ideas. Just as Steve Jobs turned his

fascination with calligraphy into an unlikely, differentiating cornerstone of the early Apple experience, Wade delivers countless insights premised on her ability to demonstrate how hard-won learning from one field can revolutionize 'the way forward' when applied in another. Embracing Progress is must reading for anyone curious about the Future of Work and the changing topography of modern life."

—JOSHUA ABRAM, FOUNDER,
NEUEHOUSE

EMBRACING
PROGRESS

EMBRACING
PROGRESS

NEXT STEPS FOR THE FUTURE OF WORK

A. SOPHIE WADE

Advantage®

Copyright © 2017 by A. Sophie Wade.

All rights reserved. No part of this book may be used or reproduced in any manner whatsoever without prior written consent of the author, except as provided by the United States of America copyright law.

Published by Advantage, Charleston, South Carolina.
Member of Advantage Media Group.

ADVANTAGE is a registered trademark, and the Advantage colophon is a trademark of Advantage Media Group, Inc.

Printed in the United States of America.

10 9 8 7 6 5 4 3 2 1

ISBN: 978-1-59932-785-3
LCCN: 2017935875

Cover and layout design by Katie Biondo.

Cartoons by Andrew Grossman at Cartoon Resource.

Alyssa Peek of Peek Photography www.peekphotography.nyc

This publication is designed to provide accurate and authoritative information in regard to the subject matter covered. It is sold with the understanding that the publisher is not engaged in rendering legal, accounting, or other professional services. If legal advice or other expert assistance is required, the services of a competent professional person should be sought.

Advantage Media Group is proud to be a part of the Tree Neutral® program. Tree Neutral offsets the number of trees consumed in the production and printing of this book by taking proactive steps such as planting trees in direct proportion to the number of trees used to print books. To learn more about Tree Neutral, please visit **www.treeneutral.com.**

TreeNeutral

Advantage Media Group is a publisher of business, self-improvement, and professional development books. We help entrepreneurs, business leaders, and professionals share their Stories, Passion, and Knowledge to help others Learn & Grow. Do you have a manuscript or book idea that you would like us to consider for publishing? Please visit **advantagefamily.com** or call **1.866.775.1696.**

To Liam and Gigi,

You started me on this journey to be a catalyst for a better world of work. I am passionate about the prospect of your being able to enjoy your "work-lives." I am profoundly grateful for your understanding when I was consumed with writing this book.

TABLE OF CONTENTS

ABOUT THE AUTHOR
WHY ME?

I research, write, consult, and speak regularly about the "Future of Work"—an umbrella term that encompasses the many areas where work-related changes are being experienced and many more are anticipated. My intention in communicating widely about topics in this field is to help bring clarity and direction, as well as share advice and tips. The goal of this book, along with some humor to add levity, is to do the same.

I think I have always been excited about what's ahead and what's new. Perhaps it's the "geek" in me. I am comfortable with change, and I love to learn. My approach is to absorb and analyze, then permit myself some distance to enable me to understand—whether I then choose to embrace the new idea or information or not. Presented with new data, I also review legacy situations to consider what affect the new information might have and whether reframing of current or past or future issues, habits, and circumstances is warranted. This process has served me well when tackling the Future of Work.

The prevailing and anticipated challenges that we all face in effecting smooth transitions to the new ways of working are considerable. Much is changing around us and will continue to evolve for the foreseeable future. My experiences working in five countries— across Europe, Asia, and the United States—are useful as a bank of information to draw from in order to deconstruct and understand the range of scenarios we are moving from and to. With operational understanding from a wide variety of cultural situations, working attitudes, and formats, I learned early on that subjective judgments undermine comprehension and prevent fruitful communication, collaboration, and progress.

Furthermore, my own career has been **latticed** (all bold terms can be found in the lexicon at the back of the book) and diverse—foreshadowing the current career paradigm shifts. After switching from science and mathematics to study Chinese at Oxford University, I started my career in Hong Kong. In pre-email times, rather expensive telephone calls were the only way to communicate with my parents back in the U.K. I was therefore mostly left to my own devices to determine my path. Had I been back in London, the influence of more "traditional" ways of thinking—rather than the basic logic that I used—would likely have determined a different career course for me.

I followed a media-/technology-industry continuum and traversed sectors—satellite, telecoms, Internet—diagonally rather than pursuing a "vertical" singular discipline and standard single-sector trajectory. I leveraged and advanced my skills in many different fields and moved around the world gathering beneficial new experiences—in a very Millennial-like manner!

After almost two decades doing financially-focused strategic development—helping companies raise financing, build their business, or create new internal business initiatives—I made a major transition in my career. My daughter was three at the time and my son was ten, and they were asking me to work less or get a "half job" so that I could spend more time with them. So, in 2010, I sought a way to combine an interesting job that I could be deeply engaged in, that paid well, *and* that would allow me more time and attention for my family and household-related activities. It was an almost delusional objective at that point!

Specific job solutions were few and far between. Instead, after reading Sylvia Ann Hewlett's 2007 book *Off-Ramps and On-Ramps*, I recognized that greater flexibility in the workplace would help me create my desired working circumstances. This was the catalyst for the birth of my own company, Flexcel Network, in 2011. Flexcel Network was originally focused on workplace flexibility—advocating for it as well as educating, connecting, and introducing people and companies looking to leverage the wide range of flexible working models.

I had found my passion.

It was timely. Over the next couple of years, a confluence of events occurred, starting with the publication of Anne-Marie Slaughter's article "Why Women Still Can't Have It All" in *The Atlantic* in 2012, along with Marissa Mayer's appointment as CEO of Yahoo with her subsequent canceling of all teleworking options, and then Sheryl Sandberg's book *Lean In* and Arianna Huffington's first Thrive conference in 2013. While these were not all positive occurrences, and with much focus on women in the workplace, together they shone a spotlight on workplace issues and increased recognition of the limitations of the prevailing working models.

The result was much public- and private-sector debate about what flexible working options were available, what might and "should" be offered, and current real or perceived consequences of potential widespread adoption that might warrant attention and addressing. Workplace flexibility was finally getting real attention, and some real progress followed—acknowledgment, understanding, and then action.

In my constant reading of the latest published research and relevant articles to promote the increasingly-widespread positive impact of flexible working implementation and new types of customized benefits, I noticed that many other interrelated and interdependent areas were also evolving in a meaningful way. The framework of the Future of Work emerged and captured many of these aspects. I then recognized that workplace flexibility is but one of the core issues actually at play. The full gamut ranges from purpose-driven culture and engagement to empathetic leadership and personalized working, from distributed authority and flatter hierarchy to diversified careers, career-experience management, and activity-based working environments—along with the deep technology integration that transforms and supports it all. The revelation made a profound impact on me.

I had already seen how challenging it can be for individual professionals to design a new **working profile** for themselves, when they have been so used to staying within the confines of an inflexible system. I had asked hundreds of people over the course of a few years to describe their optimal work setup, and almost no one coming from a full-time, fixed corporate job could begin to express their choices. I had also assisted companies that had been similarly tested when trying to implement workplace flexibility successfully and adjust for each employee as an individual.

On the other side, a major investment bank announced that it was introducing workplace flexibility with the specific goal of attracting more women. Internally, however, the policies were not communicated in detail or genuinely-supported by senior management firm-wide, which employees soon recognized. Consequently, they were fearful even to talk about relevant options, let alone take advantage of them. Without cultural acceptance and authentic execution, not only did the bank not achieve the rewards it desired from implementing the new policy, but the employees were frustrated, as they felt unable to benefit from it. This happens all too frequently.

I recounted many similar stories and situations while having lunch with the founder of 85 Broads (now Ellevate Network), Janet Hanson, who has been somewhat of a mentor. I was most concerned about the challenges of so many changes ahead. With her career experience working at Lehman Brothers and Goldman Sachs, Hanson pointed out that large corporations would really benefit from assistance in adapting to all these changes. I realized that my comprehension of both corporate *and* employee perspectives would be extremely valuable in facilitating the transition of companies and their employees with as little disruption as possible.

I then focused my attention and my company on the Future of Work and on supporting evolution to the new digitally-transformed and talent-focused integrated working environment. Since then, it has been both fascinating and demanding—first to comprehend fully what is involved and then to execute successfully upon appropriate changes identified.

Perhaps the most important point to appreciate is that *every* situation—every company and its combination of specific jobs, workers, and relationships—is unique. Furthermore, the breadth and depth of the impact of the different elements is also specific to each organization, and their interdependent nature is complex.

No matter where you are in the process of transitioning your company for the Future of Work, I hope this book will be helpful as a resource and tool. The environment is constantly evolving, and the more information, examples, and ideas you have access to, the better you can support and augment your efforts to develop strategies and define and refine plans to implement new ways of working. In this way, you will have a greater opportunity to roll-out a working environment for your company that will allow it to thrive in the years to come.

FOREWORD

BY PIP COBURN, FOUNDER, COBURN VENTURES

I find Sophie Wade to be extraordinary. In my study during the past twenty-plus years, I have come to believe that generating monumental change may require heavy doses of strong intention, significant exertion, and great skill. Sophie has massive quantities of all three.

How she got this way I don't know. I suspect by age five she wanted to know everything she could about the world and likely drove her parents crazy with all her questions! I also suspect this was tolerable because her intent to share what she learned to make the world a better place was so clear. Creating several careers and becoming a true global citizen before I had ever heard the phrase also likely added to the recipe.

Sophie knows there isn't just one path. She understands complexity and confusion. With this in mind, if you have a deep intention to nurture a robust, adaptable, healthy, dynamic, responsive organization filled with grace, you are likely in the right place.

In many ways "business" has been used as a justification for the opposite! For many around the globe "business" means it's okay to act out of alignment with deeply-held values because "it's just business." The lines of "work" and "personal" have blurred. While that may create downside, one extraordinary benefit is that the contradictions and justifications and excuses that were allowable in how someone chose to carry themselves in "business" vs. "personal" perhaps don't feel very good anymore. When you only worked at the office, the kids wouldn't have a chance to overhear your "aggressive" negotiating tactics. But in the living room or the soccer sidelines or at the beach, a double-life will be revealed. Perhaps this always-available blurring has some thinking twice.

"Inaction *is* a choice."

It is. There are so many books that write coercively that you *must* change! But so far as I can tell, at the individual or organizational level, inaction *is* very much a choice. Well, it may be a choice for most but not for some.

There are a group of people out there I like to call "Road Makers" who cannot help themselves but to pour heart, soul, and entire being into creating a better world. Inaction isn't a choice for them. Their energy must go somewhere. They see possibility, and they are compelled from deep inside to act. It is often lonely. Being a Road Maker is not the easy path. But Road Makers also experience pure joy. It doesn't stop at getting out of bed quickly in the morning. They often would love to skip sleep and hyperspace to morning so they could keep at it.

Sophie Wade is such a person. When I created a very specific intimate community called Road Makers, I was so thankful that

Sophie wanted to join in and I have had the privilege to get to know her all the more. There is a pretty strong chance that you are a Road Maker as well because Road Makers tend to read books titled *Embracing Progress.*

This book will absolutely not help you make your numbers the next quarter or two. You know that. So if you are reading even this far it seems you consider a longer-term orientation as more substantive. Road Makers think that way.

I would be surprised if you don't disagree with Sophie somewhere along the line here. Sophie and I debate often, and every single time I speak with Sophie I automatically become all the more engaged in whatever it is. She inspires engagement. You may find it hard to do anything *but* engage. She is not hoping for your agreement with all her ideas. She hopes to inspire exceptional engagement.

The next generation of humans and organizations will likely pursue far greater alignment of values and actions in business and Sophie Wade provides thinking and skills to create organizations that can bring it all together to meet that demand.

ACKNOWLEDGMENTS

S o many people have contributed their ideas and support and enabled this book to become a reality—in the conversations they have had with me, the ideas they have debated, the counter arguments and concerns they have challenged me with, the insights and connections they have shared, the concepts they have exposed me to, the opportunities they have offered me, the doors they have opened for me, the time they have spent with me, and the emotional support they have given me.

I hope I have listed all of the people to whom I owe much gratitude over the past few years as I have been gathering information and intelligence. With profound appreciation, I would like to acknowledge: Joshua Abram, Vinit Bharara, Malte Barnekow, Ronit Berkman, Kenny Blatt, Matthew Bishop, Susan Bratton, Matt Breitfelder, Jennifer Brown, Gerry Cardinale, Tanya Castell, Pip Coburn, Danielle DuBoise, Jennifer Ebert, Anastasia Fischer, Stewart D. Friedman, Paula Froelich, Cynthia Greenawalt, Janet Hanson, Chason Hecht, Arianna Huffington, Julia Johnston, Placid Jover, Nathan Knight, Irwin Kula, Vijay Kumar, Dr. Jaime Levine, Jane

Maksoud, Grant McCracken, Gavin McGarry, Francine Parham, Greg Parsons, Faith Popcorn, Dee Dee Ricks, Road Makers II, Andy Serwer, Diana Sierra, Julie Silver MD, Carey Smith, Kathryn Sollman, Docks Sutherland, Lucian Tarnowski, Brynne Thompson, Whitney Tingle, Erin Weed, Maximillian Weiner, Joseph White, Karyn Zochowski, and last but not least, Alvin Toffler R.I.P.

INTRODUCTION

"WHAT'S IT LIKE, RIDING A DINOSAUR?"

This was a playful, but poignant, question posed by Steve Heyer, former president and COO of Coca-Cola and former CEO of Starwood Hotels, speaking to the CEO of a company that currently generates billions of dollars in revenues with tens of thousands of employees. Heyer wasn't joking. If a company isn't moving with the times and evolving their workplace and workforce dynamics, extinction is certainly a possibility, no matter how positive current metrics may still look.

A major insurance company in New York exemplified this in 2015. It had very strong current revenues but was having an issue hiring Millennials to build up its pool of new talent. Candidates wouldn't even get as far as the interview room. Once they reached the appropriate floor of the silent, hallowed, wood-paneled, energy-less, closed-door monolith of headquarters, they would turn on their heels and walk out. A major renovation ensued to present a more friendly and welcoming environment to encourage potential recruits to pursue the interview process.

Cosmetic changes certainly make a difference, and fluffy sofas and primary-colored furnishings can entice prospects to come in. However, that is not enough. Potential hires these days are all too aware of any discord between the physical environment and the corporate culture. So, it was critical for the company first to review and revamp old ways of working and adopt a more open and amiable approach—or hiring probability would have remained low. This step is much harder to implement but is an integral part of making progress.

However, you know that already. If you are reading this book, I am assuming you "get" it. You are already on board with the spirit of change that is in the air. You have long noticed the different energy levels and topics of discussion among employees at your company. You have realized that the same dynamics were being experienced elsewhere. You have been reading articles about **digital transformation**, purpose-driven culture, and new workforce demands. Relevant initiatives are likely already underway at your organization.

If you have a sense that the changes are for the better, then I agree with you. I imagine you have also realized that where we are going is very different from where we have been. You want to bring new thinking to your company or are looking to take the next steps, and you recognize that the route is far from straightforward. This book is here to help you understand and navigate what's ahead.

So, what's new?

Pretty much everything! In business media, webinar topics, and conference headliners, there is a growing crescendo of coverage in response to a previously-unrecognizable set of new employment demands and dynamics—flexible, personalized, happier, and more "human." The transformation is fundamental and significant—technology-enabled and talent-focused, enhancing workers' **well-being**. This is "progress."

"Believe me, I know transformation isn't easy.
I pulled a muscle once."

Some business leaders—executives and managers—are still resisting the changes. This response is neither practical nor wise. However, some are still thinking that not adapting is preferable to the significant investment of time and energy that the transition will entail—in learning, strategizing, planning, testing, and making modifications. Let's admit that inaction *is* an option—but it is a choice of stagnation, not progress, and it is best to recognize fully its implications and consequent possible trajectories. The future of businesses that are not taking action is less than clear. Which companies survive remains to be seen. Some certainly will not.

Many are in their death throes already, generally with technology- or talent-related issues, and they have limited time left to get on board. Strategic fundamental change takes time. Hesitating can be the death knell for industry incumbents, especially when digitally-integrated, agile start-ups do not have the burden of having to deconstruct and redefine legacy operations to embed technology and incorporate new ways of thinking and working.

On the other hand, here you are.

You are already moving forward—mentally and/or operationally. Your thoughtful understanding can be leveraged to bring a new mindset to your workplace or share it more widely. Armed with data evidence, guiding principles, and an understanding of what needs to be done, you can create or expand a rich working environment at your company that embraces a new concept of work and accrues the many benefits to the business and your workforce alike.

Why? You *do* understand what is going on, you *do* believe fundamentally in the powerful, positive outcomes, and you *are* prepared to do what it takes (within reason) to adapt and succeed moving forward. However, these are liminal times, and different operating parameters and dynamics are already disrupting companies all around you. It is important to have a good comprehension of the broad scope of the transformation in process so that you are not blindsided—for the future of your company, for your professional success, and for your personal fulfillment.

The change is considerable, ongoing, and pervasive—no matter what you approach first and howsoever you choose to phase and roll out modifications—and will likely be destabilizing to some extent for a good portion of your employees. So, the more transparent you can be, the better—to help them understand what, why, and how things are transitioning. This is not easy or simple, and even the most knowledgeable and pioneering folks continue to explore and experiment and constantly refine and evolve their strategies, plans, and tactics.

I have therefore sought to provide a reasonably broad view of the Future of Work in this book, as well as go into a few areas in more detail to give helpful context regarding the background and situation. It is useful first to understand more of the bigger picture and then to focus in on your particular priority, so that you can develop plans for whatever areas you may want to address now or soon. The ultimate objectives of this book are to:

- inform and give you context and encouragement;

- explain where we are and why;

- provide compelling and convincing data to increase and share understanding and help reduce others' hesitation or resistance;

- outline an effective approach for you to project your desired Future-of-Work environment; assess your current situation; and create your next steps, including measurement of your progress;

- support development of the powerful win-win situations that the new working environment truly heralds.

Not all of the ideas expressed here are mine. I have read widely, as noted earlier, as well as interviewed, spoken with, listened carefully to, and advised numerous employers, employees, and independent workers about their existing, desired, and expected Future-of-Work environments. I have discussed and debated with others who are well versed in this field. I hope to have cited every key research document that has been a core contributor to the information in this book and noted all the people whose ideas I have shared here. There are many more great ideas, predictions, stories, and insights that I could have included, and the book could be updated endlessly as the workplace changes and new ways of working continue to emerge and evolve. I had to stop somewhere.

Journey into the Future of Work

In chapter 1, "Principles, Priorities, Pillars, and People," I start by recounting our current circumstances and the reasons I am enthusiastically supporting your intent and efforts to adapt and advance. I highlight the outcomes and rewards that are extremely attainable if careful attention and worthwhile effort is applied to execute plans to transition. I unveil an approach based on first principles that emphasize four themes or "Priorities" and six "Pillars," which group the areas that need to evolve at your company to move you forward. I explain that this approach, combined with a significant focus on your talent, will help you as you start or continue to advance your company's transition. I also explain how to utilize the takeaways in each chapter.

Chapter 2, "Technology: Enabler, Driver, Supporter, Integrator," discusses technology in its different catalytic, underpinning, and influential roles. Integration is a core factor in the Future-of-Work progress. Chapter 3, "Me-llennials, We-llennials: Inclusion Matters," recognizes that an inclusive approach to any individual and generation is the only way to move forward.

Chapter 4, "The New Rules of Engagement, Culture First," addresses the pervasive issue and impact of the unenthusiastic workforce. The impact of corporate culture is discussed, as well as the importance of **personalization** to drive productivity and help attract and retain the top talent you need. Chapter 5, "Leadership: Ego and Empathy," describes new leadership characteristics that will enable your company to develop a relevant transformation plan and execute upon it effectively. New-style leaders throughout your company can then guide the organization during potentially-tumultuous times of transition.

Optimizing the productivity of your organization is the focus of chapter 6, "Productivity, Performance, and Personalization." It explains how personalization is the key to optimizing your work-force's individual contributions and describes how to approach and execute upon a talent-focused strategy. Chapter 7, "Mindset, Policies, and Environment," focuses on your company's core attitude—how it is incorporated in company policies and then expressed in the general workplace environment. The evolving external business circumstances are also raised in anticipating possible effects on your company's operating environment.

Chapter 8, "Creativity and Collaboration," details how to stimulate and support innovation, wherever your employees and contractors—both individuals and teams—are working from. In chapter 9, "Freelancers and Frameworks," I recognize and review the changing composition of the workforce, so that you can contemplate the optimal makeup of your teams over time. In addition, I propose the replacement of fixed organizational structures with flexible frameworks to allow companies to respond effectively to marketplace needs so you can look at what might be appropriate for your organization.

The changes are not without consequences for your employees, and chapter 10, "Current Conundrums: Choice and Context" looks at how you can best support their transition, reducing confusion and fear and optimizing results for all. Intergenerational circumstances are explored with a view to improving communications. Chapter 11, "Careers: Mapping and Mentoring," considers the new career landscapes and anticipates ways to work with your employees to develop their potential going forward and to retain them longer.

Chapter 12, "The Organization as a Living Organism," proposes a different way of thinking about your company—it's very "human" nature and describes the different character and feeling of evolved and evolving talent-focused corporations. Chapter 13, "Your Plan for Progress," brings it all together and proposes a framework to assist you, by leveraging first principles, to develop the strategies, plans, and tactics you need to prepare for and transform your company for the Future of Work. This includes recommendations to ensure that progress and outcomes are tracked and measured all along the way.

In the epilogue, "What Else Is Important?", I consider other notable related areas that are affecting and will affect the Future-of-Work environment, such as education, retirement, automation, the possible need for basic income, and the status of the American Dream. It's weekend reading, rather than the weekday strategic and operating guidance that comprises the rest of the book.

After that is the lexicon. We know actions matter. However, words do as well. Clumsy terminology can waste people's time with distracting argument about what the words mean. I am keen that ideas and information are clearly understood, enabling productive discussion about the issues in order to make progress. I therefore include a lexicon of the key terms that are commonly used in the wide-ranging Future-of-Work field. I include the definition that I am attributing to each word, so that my meanings are evident and unambiguous as you advance through the book.

As you plan and make progress, there will be many people who will either resist your ideas and desired changes or else need much data to convince or encourage them. There is much compelling research to support every element that I lay out in this book, so please look up the data and research references in the endnotes. These are reports and studies that I have found extremely useful, that can also help you counter or reinforce arguments, whenever required to advance your plans and projects.

Your Next Steps

Much has already been studied, understood, documented, tested, and measured, and is now being monitored, but the Future-of-Work environment is a work in progress. A few actually predicted its advent decades ago, including futurist Alvin Toffler in his seminal book *The Third Wave,* published in 1981. While it may feel like we are still in the early stages of the evolution, many of the drivers have been advancing for decades—including underlying technology components and functionality that were developed or enabled years ago. However, these have only gradually been activated, acknowledged, or utilized.

I estimate that we may just now be reaching the peak years of transition to the new working environment. The years ahead until 2030, or at least 2025, are likely to be rather turbulent—due to the number of internal changes ahead for every company, combined with many ongoing external market-related developments.

Even if these will not be the first steps towards an enriched Future-of-Work environment, the next steps on your journey to transforming your company may well represent some of the most profound adjustments yet tackled. At the same time, they will allow you to respond to the new market conditions and meet your business's and employees' needs. This much change cannot be clean and simple to implement. I often use the word "messy" to describe what's ahead. I say it's a technical term and always get a laugh. Good. Instability is scary, and there is much of that ahead. "Messy" isn't a comfortable state for many to work in or with. Nevertheless, we can all get used to it, and familiarity will reduce distraction and concern.

As noted, the information in this book is far from exhaustive. There is too much going on, too much in flux, and too much that is unknown. Every day, I observe, listen, absorb, learn, and deepen my understanding across the breadth of issues. Moreover, your company's situation is exceptional, as is every other organization's. This book aims to add significantly to what you currently know, giving you a good understanding of the range of changes that are in process or anticipated. You can then have a more informed perspective when responding to all kinds of new developments that may be impacting your business *internally*, which is the book's focus. The information here seeks to outline how to achieve a transition—it will help you understand the options, analyze your situation, and develop appropriate next steps.

As you embark on the next steps in creating your company's Future-of-Work environment, placing priority on engaging your managers and employees, personalizing your approach, and giving them more choice will get you nearly halfway there. Everyone can then rally with you to bring about meaningful integration throughout the company.

CHAPTER 1

PRINCIPLES, PRIORITIES, PILLARS, AND PEOPLE

*The existence of any method, standard, custom or practice is
no reason for its continuance when a better is offered.*

THEODORE ROOSEVELT

Sakara Life, a Manhattan-based online wellness company founded in 2012, is run by Millennial cofounders Danielle DuBoise and Whitney Tingle. Neither had much previous management experience prior to launching Sakara, and DuBoise says they consider that a "blessing in disguise."

She says: "It means we get to discover what works best for us and Sakara rather than conforming to what we learned in school or at another job. We have close advisors who help us, and we try to do what we think is right and manage in a way we'd want to be managed. We also try things out and then adapt as necessary ... We believe that each person is responsible for their own happiness. If they are not happy, then they need to do something to change things. We believe in empowering individuals—we tell them we're not here to watch your every move; we want you to be your own worst critic and create your own level of happiness and efficiency."

So far, it is working very well—Sakara is expanding quickly, delivering their products nationwide, and the founders continue to learn and adapt every day. Taking this kind of fresh and progressive approach is much easier when unburdened by legacy habits and entrenched operating practices. However, technology-accelerated market developments are pushing for change and progress and are placing new demands on companies to be more flexible and responsive.

Progress is at the heart of the American Dream. It is embedded in the vision of an America that historian James Truslow Adams described as a land where "life should be better and richer and fuller for everyone," where every individual has the opportunity for success and prosperity. However, tens of millions of American workers are neither experiencing the opportunities nor anticipating the potential realization of this dream.

Only 32 percent of American workers are engaged in their work,[1] with as much as $450 billion in lost productivity;[2] 55 percent of Americans did not use all their vacation days in 2015 with 58 percent citing lack of support from their boss as the reason;[3] 45 percent of men and 39 percent of women reported work-life conflict in 2014;[4] and non-farm business productivity declined for most of 2016.[5]

Americans have the right to the "pursuit of happiness" noted in the Declaration of Independence. They are now pushing for more of that happiness (or some equivalent or elements of it) in the workplace, where it has been sorely absent. They are demanding progress—new ways of working that can enhance their well-being by improving their lives and easing their struggles. Technological developments are now enabling new ways of working that represent the kind of progress that workers are looking for—flexible, personalized, location-independent, nonlinear, partially virtual, less hierarchical, and happier—and their employers can also benefit from them.

Truth be told, the changes are long overdue. Workers have been struggling for decades, as society's evolution since about the mid-1960s—including women's increasing involvement in the corporate workplace, the changing and more diverse family structures, and postponed retirement—has not yet been sufficiently acknowledged and adapted to. There is much pent-up demand for change to relieve the strain and struggle caused by rigid and lagging labor and employment laws. This pressure for change is combined with the technology-derived transformation and a cadre of mostly younger workers who are enthusiastically embracing and promoting long-awaited adjustments and even demanding additional adaptation. The result is significant and broad-based modifications in operating practices, as well as accompanying psychological shifts reflecting new attitudes and approaches to work.

Employers who embrace the progressive changes underway can achieve great reward and advantage if they adapt thoughtfully and expeditiously, such as by increasing engagement[6] and productivity and reducing turnover. However, with transformation occurring across so many areas—which is expected to be ongoing for a good number of years—classic change processes need updating and many established best practices are no longer valid.

For now, with the departure from traditional routines and models, coupled with situational complexity and numerous options, I believe that a focus on first principles—rather than trying to tweak habitual operating practices—is the optimal approach for determining the way forward. In stepping away from current routines, this methodology involves adopting a neutral perspective, then exploring relevant options and developing hypothetical scenarios, allowing all working constituents to contribute in meaningful ways. The greatest range of perspectives can be evaluated and incorporated if an actively-inclusive approach is taken that is as objective as possible. Starkly different viewpoints can bring the kind of alternative thinking that will help transform your company and working methodologies and achieve all the possible benefits.

In the future working environment—for which "ecosystem" is a more relevant term—each company's and each individual's position and path will be unique, interconnected, integrated, and dynamic. There are no "best practices" to effect the transition, for now at least. First principles can be used effectively to assess and sketch the range of relevant options, reviewing all the core areas that are outlined, which I streamline and group as the six "Pillars" of your organization that I will explain later on in the chapter. As you focus on these areas and your talent, I recommend you incorporate the key themes I have identified as the four "Priorities"—engagement, personalization, integration, and choice. Adaptations can then be made based on broad-based understanding, leveraging a combination of neutrally-developed hypotheses, with targeted involvement from each division, team, and, as applicable, person. Sakara's founders are effectively using first principles as their core approach, guided by the Sakara values, and layering on recent experience, intuition, and advice.

I observe that the transition is away from the impersonal, inflexible, and constrained past experiences of the twentieth century. I firmly believe that the changes afoot are, ultimately, going to transform the majority of the world's workplaces into happier, healthier, more supportive, and more engaging working environments for their workers' improved well-being, such as DuBoise describes at Sakara. The consequential and important result will be workers' increased productivity for the reciprocal benefit of companies that understand and accept the changes and adapt appropriately for their workers and businesses.

How We Got Here

Our past experiences will likely not help us forecast what is ahead, as so many elements will be neither predictable nor incremental. However, a little history is useful—and may be surprising, too—to serve as an explanation of how and why we are where we are and help remind us about the urgent need for progress, as well as the improvements that updated working models and methods will bring.

There are several aspects that can be helpful to remember if you are excited about, but also somewhat daunted by, the changes to be made, or are occasionally nostalgic about the past and traditional ways of doing things. Should there be doubt about what makes sense going forward, it can be startling to realize just how arbitrary, purposefully contrived, or simply out of date the current setup is. Consider, too, the "logic" of the ways we are still doing things, as well as the developments that are catalyzing the profound changes we are starting to witness in terms of new technology-enabled operating and working models and ensuing workforce mindsets and demands.

The Fixed Working Week: To start with, the forty-hour workweek was proposed by an important Welsh socialist named Robert Owen[7] in 1817. He came up with the concept and a catchy slogan, "Eight hours' labor. Eight hours' leisure. Eight hours' rest," which swept around the world, catalyzing new labor laws in the 1800s that brought an end to the ten- to sixteen-hour factory workdays in many countries. However, it took until 1938 to become law in the United States. So the forty-hour workweek was not created based on production-line efficiency, and it didn't specify rigidity in time or location. It was a progressive idea for changing the inhumane working conditions at the time. That's all.

Traditional Breadwinners: Key current U.S. labor and employment laws were established at an anomalous time in history. After World War II, economic policies were determinedly designed to avert possible recession and resulted in a "long boom." This was an unprecedented and probably unrepeatable period of expansion, during the 1950s and 1960s, that had lingering effects long afterwards.[8] During this period, a tight labor market born of the baby bust of the 1920s and 1930s meant that a single breadwinner could support the family and buy a home, as the median cost of housing[9] was only approximately twice the average annual income.[10] This was the unique "golden boom" time in history, when over 60 percent of women were solely working in the home[11] and when some of the more recent, important U.S. labor and employment laws were developed and enacted.

Post-boom, typical American families' working situations have changed substantially: the percentage of married couples with kids under eighteen who were dual-income households rose from 25 percent in 1960 to 60 percent in 2012; working mothers increased from below 30 percent to 70 percent in 2015; and in 40 percent of U.S. households with children under 18,[12] women are the primary or sole breadwinner, up from 11 percent in 1960.[13] The laws need updating, and workers have been struggling with inflexible employment structures that have not facilitated adaptations in response to their changing needs.

Educating the Workforce: Starting in 1790, the first factory workers in the United States were young unmarried women, as it offered them an independent income, and the men were not keen to subject themselves to the supervision of the factory owners. Prussian factory-school models from the late eighteenth and early nineteenth centuries are touted as being the prescription that solved this problem, creating schools connected to the factories that would raise generations of compliant workers. These were first adopted in Michigan and Massachusetts in 1835 and 1852, respectively.[14] Later on, in the early 1900s, Henry Ford was a major advocate of Frederick Wilson Taylor's scientific-management theory, which focused on monetary compensation and the concept that motivation resulted from payment for volume-based repetitive task work.

The effect of factory schooling was compounded by prevailing management methodologies, including Henri Fayol's popular autocratic "command and control" type theories. The American workforce was trained for the typically limited scope and employment possibilities of the factories that formed the bedrock of the emerging nation. There is now important understanding about what actually motivates workers, as well as different approaches being considered for developing children and the new skills they need for their future careers. These factors combine to catalyze and advance new ideas and solutions for education, ongoing corporate learning and development, and career planning.

Exponential Development: In 1965, Gordon Moore of Intel made his famous scientific observation[15] that predicted the exponential pace of increased power with decreased cost; this became known as Moore's Law. The first manifestation of this was widespread use of electronics and digitization, including automated production. Now, building on that with the embedding of technology into operational systems and models, and pervasive and spreading interconnectedness, we have reached a new state.

Klaus Schwab, executive chairman of the World Economic Forum, calls this new state the "Fourth Industrial Revolution," which is "building on the Third, the digital revolution . . . [the Fourth is] characterized by a fusion of technologies that is blurring the lines between the physical, digital, and biological spheres." Schwab describes its unique evolution at an "exponential rather than a linear pace."[16] Markets are evolving faster as a consequence, and the businesses that comprise them are struggling to keep up with the pace. No wonder this "revolution" is disrupting almost everyone, everywhere.

Empowered Individuals: Previously, there was an "information power pyramid," which gave disproportionate power to those placed at and near the top, who had access to the most data. Now, thanks to the Internet's extensive presence and ability to disseminate terabytes of information easily, this pyramid has all but collapsed. Extraordinary access to data, connectivity, and potent mobile-computing capabilities represent a major transfer of power toward the individual, affording each person unprecedented flexibility, reach, visibility, and voice. Each person now has much more comprehension of his or her situation relative to others—the disparities, the realities, and the alternatives.

Technology developments in mobile computing are affecting the standard employment format and practices as work evolves from being tied to a fixed time and place to becoming purely an activity. The rigid boundaries of the workplace and workday are dissolving with psychological impact as personal and professional roles blend and activities become more integrated. Further texture is added as employees are urged to "bring their whole selves to work."

The Concept of Work: The Great Recession shook people's confidence, and the instability of the recovery alerted many to the changes in their career prospects, the lower anticipated long-term rewards, and their general economic potential going forward. The reaction of many workers, of all ages, is to reevaluate the newly integrated role of work in their lives. They are moving on from the Calvinist[17] concept of work that was deliberately associated with a sense of struggle and effort, and no longer looking for the historical monetary and status-related rewards. Purpose has become a new qualifier for job seekers, especially the younger cadres,[18] as they assess the fit of their values with those of the culture of a possible new employer. The essence of work is starting to have a more positive theme associated with it.

In addition, the shift to experience and share (rather than own), to seek impact (rather than material possessions), also creates very different possibilities as to what success means for individuals and, in turn, for the organizations they work for. Permission has been granted for new, different, and much broader interpretations of what a successful career looks like and what achievements are valued. A much more personal concept of success is now becoming accepted and respected. For organizations, creating impact programs or Get One, Give One strategies (such as at TOMS®) can be an important contributor to their success, because many employees—current as well as prospective—value them highly.

Principles and Pillars

With just these few examples, it is evident that much of the evolution in process is explicable, reasonable, and/or warranted. It makes sense not to resist it but instead to work with it. Corporations built prior models using the best information available at the time—within the constraints, demands, and needs of the earlier, prevailing environments. However, the conditions those models created have not been enabling people to do their best work. Unfortunately, much of the discomfort or inefficient working circumstances stem from management mindsets and practices that are not actually appropriate for achieving optimal productivity, especially in today's working climate.

Progress is a natural desire and inevitable direction. The fixed forty-hour workweek and gray and grim cubicle-grid offices are fading, replaced by flexible days and locations with brighter, more colorful, varied, activity-based workplace settings. In fact, simply put, the new ways of working are mostly about making practical changes that make sense to engage employees, improve their well-being,[19] boost productivity, and operate more effectively, resulting in a more vibrant and dynamic corporate ecosystem.

Nonetheless, the changes are plentiful, multifaceted, and pervasive. Critical areas concern technology integration—potentially disrupting core business models and processes—and engaging talent, particularly through personalization and choice. Personalization and choice present compelling changes, but ones that typically entail significant new back-end operating support. Much of this is already being provided by sophisticated software, but some important HR technology is still emerging or yet to be defined or developed.

The customization and complexity that is involved with the current phase of the Future-of-Work evolution means that there are no cookie-cutter models for you to select from and implement and no simple rules or best practices for you to follow. Furthermore, the substantial changes expected are hard to plan for without being tempted to edit current strategies and tactics.

Unless your company is small and/or less than five years old, I believe that devising incremental extensions or adaptations to current practices will not result in strategic transformational change. Linear and legacy thinking will not facilitate your bringing truly dynamic and flexible, individualized and integrated new models and practices to your company. To some extent, your role is as a catalyst to "disrupt" or "hack" your own organization—carefully and thoughtfully!

How? To take the next steps, with a view to creating ideas that explore non-incremental opportunities for your company, I recommend you use *first principles*. This approach is simple in concept, while allowing you also to:

- welcome contributions encompassing a wide range of perspectives;

- incorporate the numerous elements that are part of the overall Future-of-Work evolution;

- develop a series of possible future scenarios from a neutral standpoint;

- select relevant options to adapt for your specific current business and company situation;

- remain flexible in a constantly evolving environment and focus on the objectives.

The first step is to read the first twelve chapters of this book, contributing to and confirming your solid understanding of the core elements and the prospective evolution that is anticipated for the Future of Work. In chapter 13, I take you through a process to apply this approach and develop your plan for progress. To summarize for now, the idea is that before you can step forward, you take a step back. I recommend that you create circumstances so that you can conduct brainstorming exercises with the help of others, from inside and outside your organization, where you can distance yourselves mentally (physically, too, may help in the process), as far as possible from your business.

When you step back from how the business is run today and examine the fundamental "truths" of how your business could operate optimally, in the short term and projecting much further into the future, you will be able to contemplate a very new vision for your Future-of-Work environment. I propose that in order to develop this projection, or "**future sketch**," you go through the areas, grouped as the Pillars that support the platform of your organization.

I have identified and grouped the most important areas to form the Pillars of: Technology; Culture and Mindset; Leadership, Transparency, and Hierarchy; Productivity, Performance, and Creativity; Policies, Frameworks, and Environment; and Careers, Freelancers, and Learning. Each of these areas will likely see substantial evolution as your company transitions to a new working framework and operating practices. For example, you consider your culture and contemplate where you want it to be in the future—how articulated, understood, and communicated-in comparison to current circumstances.

As you review the Pillars, and the areas that comprise them, the focus is on your talent and ensuring attention to the four Priorities of engagement, personalization, integration, and choice; incorporating data; and understanding trends and the ongoing evolution. Once you have composed the vision, combining future sketches from each area, then it is a question of specifically understanding your current company status in each area. At this point, you will be in a position to explore the most beneficial possible routes toward your desired future environment and, consequently, to create appropriate plans and start to trial them. Change will be continuing, so there is actually no fixed destination, per se. Instead, this will be an ongoing exercise, repeated at regular intervals so that you can make relevant adjustments as you progress.

All of the Pillar areas as well as the Priorities are described in the following chapters, together with new ideas, methodologies, and ways to approach and support development of your plans for progress. In addition, the takeaways at the end of each chapter summarize such things as: key aspects to reflect upon when considering a first-principles approach and how the Priorities may be addressed. In addition, I suggest questions to help you evaluate your company's current status for the Pillar areas concerned in the chapter and, importantly, what metrics you can use to measure your company's progress in transition to the desired future environment, as well as for ongoing monitoring.

So, how does the first-principles approach work in practice? Taking public examples will help to illustrate the transformation that reviewing the fundamental business elements or using alternative thinking can cause in business models in the same sector. Let's look at car services—many people are familiar with this example of technology integration disrupting traditional business models.

There had long been market demand for an option other than either hailing a cab in the street or calling to book a much more expensive car service. When it was raining or rush hour or during the shift-turnover period, there used to be few cars available without a significant delay. There had been incremental technology-based improvements—most taxis could be paid by credit card, and many had TVs in the back, disseminating news, information, and entertainment. Meantime, black-limousine car services started emailing and then texting driver information to improve services, but it still required a phone call to speak to a person to reserve a car, often well in advance. However, the basic issues remained the same, and customers were often not well served.

Then along came Uber, which took a very different approach and did not attempt to make incremental improvements to the existing models. Instead, the consideration was how to maximize efficiency and convenience for the customers, so they could hail all cars in the area themselves, exactly when they wanted them. Revolutionary. Leveraging software, the Uber application became the dispatcher and completely disrupted the established business models.

I acknowledge that there are many other aspects to discuss about Uber's disruptive approach and evolving business model, some of which I will address later in the book. In this case, the example serves to illustrate the power of alternative thinking in taking a step back from the way a business or sector has traditionally operated. With a first-principles approach, you can ask "how would customers *really* be best served?" Such thinking can yield very different solutions and business models to current operations.

Progress in times of great change can be challenging—identifying and charting a direction, then navigating ahead and keeping on course—especially when the destination is not fixed. Specific hindrances to advancement can certainly be identified—for example just the abundance of choices that the Future of Work represents. Where to go, what direction to take, and how not to be distracted as different elements in different areas evolve at different times and speeds? It can become paralyzing, and the new constant is change itself. This is why I have chosen four specific themes to concentrate on—the four Priorities: engagement, personalization, integration, and choice. These are at the heart of the Future-of-Work transformation. Three of them are intertwined and focus squarely on your talent.

The Talent Agenda

You may have noticed from all the previous elements that the "grand theme" of the Future of Work is "talent"—your workers, who are finally recognized as both the brains of your organization and the energy that fuels its future and success. In the faster and more competitive marketplace, increasing the productivity—the creativity and output—of your workers is essential, as well as enabling them to be responsive to rapidly changing conditions and requirements by encouraging flexible attitudes and ways of working.

So, when you contemplate how to address your company's talent agenda using first principles, consider the culture, mindset, and values that are relevant for your company and that will nurture and support your existing employees' well-being—and attract new talent. Who do you need to hire, engage, and retain to drive your company's accomplishments in the future working environment and marketplace, and how can that best be accomplished? In developing your answers, you will be starting the transformation to an organization with a strategic talent focus.

Employees are the heart and soul of a company's culture. As the talent agenda rises in importance, so too does the "identity" of an organization. Corporate values and purpose contribute significantly to the company's identity and are key in new strategies to attract, engage, and retain talent, so that employees are well-aligned with the company's vision and goals and therefore working enthusiastically to achieve them.

Of course, the talent of any organization is made up of individuals, and the new emphasis on the talent agenda is personalization, which means enabling each and all of them to achieve their particular singular and combined potential. A new type of leader is emerging who most easily understands, manages, and motivates employees in this new working environment. The emphasis is on pull, not push; on strengths, not weaknesses; on dynamic and not static models; on leveraging each worker's expertise, independent of hierarchy; and on encouraging workers' ongoing learning and development. These elements are well represented in DuBoise's description of the approach she and Tingle use for listening to and leading their employees. They also clearly communicate Sakara's "one-team" mentality, where no job is too small for anyone, where they all eat together, reinforcing their values and the flat hierarchy, where they lead from within.

In older companies with more established and traditional operating methods, supporting employees during the transition to a new working environment is critical. Visions of careers spent mechanically climbing the ladder of a single corporation—where all eyes were fixed on the bonus package and striving to escape from cubicle to corner office—are fading. However, for many older employees, there are still few visions of the future workplace they can relate to—i.e., ones that aren't open-plan, strewn with foosball tables, and furnished with red and yellow puffy chairs!

Descriptions of collaborative workplaces like Sakara's are becoming better known. These are spaces where well-articulated values and/or a sense of purpose create a coherent culture and stimulate creativity; individuals are better understood and recognized; careers are more experiential; workweeks are less rigid; and digital platforms and tools are well integrated and utilized. The concepts sound good, but many corporations have not begun to take action or communicate the potential of these future scenarios, so their employees are uncertain and concerned.

The prospect of change generates some fear in most people. It is a natural human reaction. There is comfort and stability in routine, no matter how challenging the situation actually is. The new environment is inherently dynamic, and, driven by accelerating technological advances, there is no anticipation that the pace will let up anytime soon. However, using first principles, you can continue to be focused on the future sketch as a core strategic objective you have set, while parameters and tactics may evolve, even substantially, over time.

At the same time, the psychological framework of the new operating environment is very different. There can be agreed-upon objectives, but methods and plans to accomplish them and metrics—including key performance indicators (KPIs)—that are used to monitor them may need updating during the course of each year. The concept of moving goalposts may feel confusing or frustrating to some or, worse, destabilizing. Dealing with the uncertain or unknown is perhaps the most troubling of all circumstances to face, as it is hard to plan or prepare for.

However, there is no hurdle to help people over. Part of adapting for the Future of Work is assisting people to make a mental shift to recognize and adjust to the new reality of constant change. This is where grounding your company's workforce through their connection to a strong corporate culture can be extremely valuable. Immutable and timeless core values can serve as important anchors when the landscape is moving.

We're All in It Together

Despite the challenges ahead, I believe it is far from doom-and-gloom, because there are abundant new frontiers of opportunity ahead. Remember, this is certainly not the first time corporations have found themselves at something of a revolutionary crossroads. No employer or employee is alone in trying to adapt to the changes, either. Even pioneering organizations are experimenting and exploring, testing what works and what doesn't, and moving forward tentatively, with a very appreciative workforce where modifications are implemented with the intention to make progress.

This book will help you assess the full scope of the landscape in flux, as well as understand how we got here. After reading it, you will be better equipped both to persuade those around you and to demonstrate the benefits of an open-minded attitude, expounding the benefits of embracing progress and the rewards of new ways of working with a focus on engagement, personalization, integration, and choice. A positive, solutions-based, metrics-monitored approach is important, with dedication to an integrated execution plan to achieve optimal overall results.

The principles, Priorities, and Pillars involved in your pursuit of progress will help you achieve the better working environment you want for your people and get employees' support and energy to help your company advance. There is much to be done to transition effectively for the long term, so I will keep reminding you why taking the next steps to adapt for the Future of Work is the only viable choice and moving ahead thoughtfully and quickly!

As you progress through the chapters, please review the takeaways to support your embracing of a Future-of-Work approach, to address the questions that will arise and develop the answers that will follow. I recommend starting with an open mind, and the assumption that *anything* is possible, and *nothing* is off the table.

Chapter 1 Takeaways

- **First Principles**: The recommended methodology for the fundamental reworking and non-incremental change that is anticipated for many areas and elements relating to Future-of-Work transformation. This approach enables creation of hypothetical scenarios that are separate from and neutral to current company circumstances, in order to be as objective as possible with regard to legacy habits and practices.

- **Priorities**: Engagement, Personalization, Integration, and Choice—the four themes proposed for review and thoughtful development to advance your company through the next steps of its Future-of-Work transition.

- **Pillars**: Groupings of critical internal areas involved in your company's Future-of-Work transformation next steps:

  1. Technology.

  2. Culture and Mindset.

  3. Leadership, Transparency, and Hierarchy.

4.   Productivity, Performance, and Creativity.

5.   Policies, Frameworks, and Environment.

6.   Careers, Freelancers, and Learning.

Each Pillar is reviewed relative to the Priorities, and recommendations are proposed.

- **Evaluation**: Chapter takeaways list sample questions to ask in order to determine your company's current status with respect to specific progress-related Priorities and Pillars. Assessment is approached from a variety of angles and using multiple relevant quantitative and qualitative data points. This broad array of data will enable you first to establish a baseline from which all Future-of-Work adaptations will be assessed and then track progress as you advance.

- **Metrics**: Takeaways suggest ways to identify and/or develop appropriate metrics—or simply suggest examples—for gauging and monitoring your company's progress related to each Priority and Pillar. This data is important for measuring both your company's transition towards a desired Future-of-Work environment and its ongoing progression as circumstances continue to change.

- **Terminology**: In evolutionary times, clear understanding and communication is critical. Please refer to the lexicon at the end of the book for any key terms—identified in boldface the first time they are mentioned—for which you are not sure of the meaning, OR to clarify the specific meaning ascribed to particular terms for the purposes of explanations in this book.

CHAPTER 2

TECHNOLOGY: ENABLER, DRIVER, SUPPORTER, INTEGRATOR

The more complex and variable a system becomes, the more flexibility and variety it requires to respond effectively.
ASHBY'S LAW OF REQUISITE VARIETY

Maestro Health was founded by Rob Butler, its CEO, to improve—significantly—the existing dynamics of benefits provision and management in the employee-sponsored health-care sector through delivery of modern technology featuring personalized services. The company's health and benefits platform leverages the power of technological advances to cater to the individual needs of the HR manager along with employees' benefits needs on an individual basis. The application provides service to each HR manager customized both in content and accessibility on their preferred platform and/or device. Sophisticated software allows Maestro Health to disrupt blanket approaches and deliver compelling relevant services to end users. These services are, in turn, driving strategic and tactical operational change in the benefits sector—clients' employees are now able to take advantage of solutions tailored to them specifically. These are therefore more relevant, available, and useful to the consumer as well as being cost effective for the employer to deliver. Technology is a driver and enabler of Future-of-Work solutions here.

Fuze, another tech company, is leveraging technology as a supporter of emerging Future-of-Work environments. Fuze provides communications and application-based services to connect and enable the seamless and fruitful interactions of various combinations of office-based and distributed workers. The company first offered then-pioneering telephone and fax services overlaid on traditional landline systems to facilitate new entrepreneurial ventures' efficient operations and growth with affordable and flexible communications services. Fuze has evolved to deliver a variety of data services, intelligent software, and platform applications with seamless video, voice, and messaging services for individuals and groups. These provide critical support for the collaboration and talent-management needs of the evolving workplace, where employees and contingent workers are increasingly physically-dispersed and need to interconnect, interact, and brainstorm seamlessly.[20]

Chason Hecht is CEO of Retensa. He founded the company to focus on solving turnover issues by reviewing companies' talent lifecycle. To make a diagnosis, the software is integrated into the work- and talent-management process, where it monitors and evaluates the entire employee experience. It looks at the lifecycle of an employee from beginning to end to track how each key milestone is handled—from onboarding and getting a promotion, through being assigned a major project, all the way to separation and exit interview. Using these data points, Retensa is able to identify problem areas and highlight where to concentrate attention in order to improve employee interactions, support, and retention. When integrated effectively into relevant ongoing core operations, Retensa's software acts like a "corporate Fitbit," monitoring the pulse and overall health of the organization, and can identify issues before they become problems. Retensa is part of the wave of increasingly integrated technology that enables companies to develop and engage employees more efficiently and effectively.

Digital transformation is playing a, if not *the*, major role in the Future-of-Work evolution. Without "geeking out," it is important to appreciate the fundamental reshaping of the overall business landscape. Technology plays multiple roles—as enabler, driver, and supporter—with the consequent pervasive embedding and integration of technology throughout almost every company and the network of companies, vendors, and partners in and around a sector. The increasingly extensive presence of networked digital devices means a widespread interconnectedness that is having a huge impact on the marketplace, opportunities, transactions, and communications and is inexorably driving progress forward.

At the local level, technological advances have been enabling overdue amendments to workplace dynamics, as well as becoming drivers and catalysts for additional operational disruption. Digital developments are also supporting and enhancing new ways of working and generating solutions for new back-end services. The disruption is substantial and ongoing. If your company has not already taken meaningful steps to review how and where technology can be

integrated to optimize—potentially by fundamentally changing—
your business models and operations, then I recommend you place it
at or close to the top of your priority list.

Digital Disruption

Technology is enabling adaptations that respond to society's evolution
over the past few decades. At the same time, technology advances are
driving new, unanticipated change. At the highest level, the intercon-
nection of billions of "technologically active" items around the world
that all gather, transmit, and share elements of data, the "Internet of
Things" (IoT), is gathering momentum and heralding innumerable
new possibilities. Having surpassed more than six billion Internet-
connected things in 2016, the IoT is anticipated to grow to over
twenty billion things by 2020.[21] The potential insights and use of
the "big data" now being collected, in combination with the latest
progress in artificial intelligence, could be remarkable, especially
considering that data-center IP (Internet protocol) traffic has been
forecast to grow at a compound annual growth rate (CAGR) of 27
percent from 2015 to 2020, exceeding fifteen zettabytes annually.
(One zettabyte is one trillion gigabytes).[22]

More immediately, the practical effect of digitization, with
powerful mobile computers (i.e. smart phones) in the hands of over
68 percent of Americans,[23] is enabling the realization of long-awaited
modifications to employment models to catch up with societal progression. The ability to work flexibly, remotely, affordably, and easily
is relieving the challenges of time-constrained office-based work
limitations.

At the same time, technology has moved from communications-
heavy functionality to becoming deeply-integrated into core business

processes. Corporate technology teams, populated with more strategic and business-savvy staff, are now becoming champions of other divisions' needs, such as sales or marketing.[24] They are working backwards into the technological requirements, including cross-functional deployment, as more business leaders are starting to work across divisions and departments, sharing ideas and data. The objective of breaking down internal corporate barriers is to identify and enable optimal work processes and reduce end-user friction as much as possible.

The result of the strategic implanting of technology into operations is often to disrupt or significantly redefine business models or processes that have been long-established and were perhaps ripe for a fresh approach, new logic, or efficiencies. Examples include cloud-based software applications, like Slack, which enable distributed workers to share, collaborate, and interact easily on projects. Amazon delivering packages to rural addresses by drone is another technology-based business model disruption, as the company starts to become involved in the last mile of transporting their goods. This is the digital transformation that will be important for reasonably-established businesses to work on as soon as possible. The IDC FutureScape Report published in November 2016[25] predicted that 70 percent of Global 500 companies will have digital transformation and innovation teams in place by the end of 2017.

Systematic Supporter

Previous use of technology—such as audio and video conferencing and remote VPN dial-in—to bridge gaps with traveling employees or distant vendors and partners has transitioned to the need to facilitate daily dialog and collaboration with a significant and growing number of remote internal and external workers:

- Twenty to twenty-five percent of the U.S. workforce now teleworks at some frequency.[26]

- Regular work-at-home grew by 103 percent between 2005 and 2015 (among those not self-employed). [27]

- Fifty-three million people—34 percent of the U.S. workforce[28]— are now doing freelance work in the United States.

There is a fundamental shift occurring in the traditional concept of "the office" and who is working where and when and how. Employees are being given more choice, including in their work environment and location, in order to stimulate engagement and, thence, productivity. The new, increasingly-dispersed workforce is enabled, as well as optimally-managed and monitored, significantly differently from fixed, office-based employees. Furthermore, in new activity-based office settings, workers can utilize a variety of different group and individual stations to complete their tasks, and these all need appropriate technology support as well.[29]

The workforce is therefore more mobile, dispersed daily to differing degrees, working from random and scattered locations in addition to office sites, whether part or full time. Employees not based in the office or at one permanent workstation perform at their best when they are well connected and highly communicated with, and their assigned tasks are transparently shared, clearly defined, and trackable,[30] which I describe further in chapters 6 and 8. A variety of devices, applications, and platforms can now cater to these needs, also taking advantage of customized software to address the new, individualized approach to employees. This is in addition to the larger numbers of independent contractors who are both being incorporated in office-based teams as well as being accessed remotely, as explained further in chapter 9.

Personalized applications can be powerful for employers and employees alike. Fuze is one of the companies providing software that allows employees to express themselves in their own individual ways, such as speech to text, if preferred. In parallel, sophisticated new software can monitor workers, understand them better, learn their habits, and adjust to optimize usage. For example, the software can help track productivity based on how many calls people make or their interactions with an application, or it can promote efficiency by suggesting short-term tasks in daily "whitespace" micro-times. (These are short time segments when a few email responses might be written and sent.)

It is imperative for employers to adopt a systematic approach to the way they digitally-enable employees. Otherwise, companies can be undermined by what is called "shadow IT." This term refers to increasingly common scenarios where employees use consumer applications to interact, instead of the company's enterprise applications, which can generate major security risks. These days, people are demanding easy-to-use business tools. They have been spoiled by an explosion of consumer applications that have made communications appear seamless, so employees may default to using Apple's FaceTime rather than dealing with an enterprise video conferencing solution, which still takes almost fifteen minutes to set up!

The Next Step Is Integration

Future-of-Work environments are exhibiting operating practices that are significantly different from legacy ones, hence the use of the word "transformation"—digital, as well as in the cultural and management realms—with many implications at corporate and personal levels. When applications are leveraged and embedded into core operations, business models and processes are often altered or can be created afresh by sector newcomers:

- Uber's software acts as the virtual dispatcher for those fulfilling the drives—fundamentally changing the process of hiring and dispatching car or project services.

- Driverless cars use embedded technology to govern most aspects of the vehicle's maneuvering and operations rather than using the traditional "support" of a human as the driver/operator.

- Retensa's software application substantially changes the methods and means used to monitor employees' work experience, diagnose issues, and manage retention.

To achieve digital transformation, it is important to create the neutral circumstances conducive to applying the first-principles approach. Then you can evaluate how technology might be the strategic driver of and catalyst for potentially-profound and lasting change in your business, in the short term and over time. The embedding of technology is not just about "vertical" integration of technology into the corporate core; it is also "horizontal" across divisions and departments. Technology facilitates the move to more flexible and responsive corporate frameworks, as outlined in chapter 9, working collaboratively and sharing data across functional areas utilizing different platforms and tools to interconnect teams and individual workers, virtually and physically.[31]

Integration is also the critical vision behind the intention to have human resources, information technology, and facilities management departments collaborate closely.[32] Later chapters will discuss different aspects of the involvement of these three groups in creating a consistent employee experience—flowing seamlessly with a coherent message and approach—from mental to virtual, and throughout the physical workplace environment. The objective is for employees and nonemployee workers alike to be able to work comfortably and seamlessly, in groups and individually, at their workstations as well as in other settings and remote locations, in order to optimize their productivity.

Another key area of technology integration is the finance department, where digitization and its big-data impact is allowing information to be gathered from and about all aspects of corporate operations. This is leading to both new processes and new effectiveness in inter-department understanding and cooperation. In addition, finance departments have improved strategic understanding of different divisions' progress and developments.[33]

In relation to the talent agenda, for the Future-of-Work environment, the use of technology is allowing each person to engage, collaborate, contribute effectively and efficiently according to their responsibilities, and be communicated with, monitored, and managed to the level necessary no matter where they are. New technology means that individual employees' needs can be met according to their personal preferences, allowing for new choices of roles, working styles, and communications means or applications. Some people prefer texting to sending emails, while others like video communication rather than audio, or prefer one collaboration or project management application over another. Distributed workers can be interconnected effectively, leveraging customizable and integrated networked platforms and applications.

For many aspects of the technology integration, incremental changes are unlikely to be sufficient to create the new strategic plans that will enable your business to be successful in the emerging working environment. There are simply too many elements to be updated and reworked, such that in combination they represent a significant departure from current circumstances. Moreover, history is not going to be relevant for anticipating what is next when so much is evolving and interdependent at the same time.

"Uh oh, the new economy is pulling away from us."

The first-principles approach can allow you to conduct a review of the fundamental elements that comprise the future objectives of your business, considering what optimal current and future products or services could look like and how these goals might be accomplished. First, consider what the "dream technology" might be that could facilitate creating and delivering them, and then I recommend following up with careful research, as these technical capabilities may well already exist. The key is to distance yourself from established practices and legacy context in order to review and analyze the fundamental tenets, components, and aims of your business. Embrace inputs from younger employees, whose lives and ways of thinking already incorporate technology at a fundamental level.

As irreverent as it might seem, "hacking" might be a concept for your company to use to conceive new ways of working. For example, bringing together programmers, software designers, and graphic artists to create new products in so-called "hackathons" has achieved some notable success for companies such as Facebook, AT&T, and Cisco Systems. This alternative approach can be applied to disrupt and rethink many areas, from product development to specific business processes, talent management, and workplace environments.[34]

It is worth noting the different effect of new technical and operational capabilities at younger companies when they are incorporated from the outset and traditional methodologies or routines do not have to be unwound or unlearned. These start-ups are creating some of the broader-level disturbance, as they are able to launch with new or projected needs and objectives and are unconstrained by legacy systems and processes when developing solutions. Uber is a simple example, as mentioned in chapter 1, shaking up the entire limousine service industry sector as a result. So, if you don't galvanize your company's Future-of-Work transition and "hack" your own business model, a start-up that may be out of your line of sight right now may well do it first and leave you scrambling to catch up.

Stepping back from legacy systems, where much time and energy has been invested and routines formed, and trying to comprehend the potential applicability and impact of very different new technologies is neither simple nor easy. Strategic thinkers in your IT department, or whomever you include in developing new plans, will be critical for successful ideation, vetting, planning, and implementation. Use first principles to observe and consider technology's different roles—driving and enabling workplace changes, supporting aspects of the new ways of working, and then creating a new paradigm based on integration, interaction, and interdependency.

Chapter 2 Takeaways

- **First Principles**: Considering the fundamental components, brainstorm or "hack" how your company's products or services might optimally be developed and delivered and operations run, especially relating to talent. Assess how—and what—technology could best achieve these and other key strategic and operational goals.

- **Priorities**:

  - Engagement—Review how specific, relevant engagement goals and initiatives (see chapter 4) can be executed and facilitated utilizing technology in multiple ways—particular platforms, applications, etc.

  - Personalization—Technology is a key facilitator for enabling the individual customization of talent-related initiatives, adjustments, and benefits.

  - Integration—Technology-wise, this is the "holy grail" for the Future-of-Work environment, involving the seamless combination and incorporation of numerous technical elements. This objective also includes gathering and using data within and across business units to inform and improve numerous aspects of strategic development and operations expeditiously.

  - Choice—It is important to weigh the numerous technology options carefully in terms of their complexity, adaptability over time, ease of implementation and integration, and more. Expert advice is beneficial when future-proofing your technology-related decisions. Furthermore, employees respond differently to talent-facing technology and device options, so soliciting their input is wise.

- **Evaluation**:

  □ How is technology being leveraged to optimize achievement of your company's objectives?

  □ To what degree are cloud-based tools and technologies being used to support distributed operations and mobile and remote workers?

  □ Have new artificial-intelligence capabilities been considered?

  □ Is "shadow IT" a concern for your IT department?

  □ How up-to-date are the applications that your workforce is using?

  □ How old is the data that is being used to inform the majority of executive and management decisions?

  □ To what degree are departments enabling and sharing information—whether internally- or externally-generated data?

  □ How seamlessly are remote and office-based workers able to collaborate using technology?

- **Metrics**: Technology will be pervasive, so metrics will likely be numerous. Careful consideration is recommended to ensure relevance for specific areas in your company. Each division and department can be tasked with identifying the specific data that will be most appropriate for measuring its progress, which may evolve over time. For example, a metric may be monitoring the extent of implementation and then might transition to tracking actual usage. For the finance department, this might be related to real-time data gathering and usage. For HR, this might include the percentage increase in the number of video-enabled meetings per week between dispersed team members, and the increase in the average number of personalized benefits signed up for and used by employees, followed by usage rates.

CHAPTER 3

ME-LLENNIALS,
WE-LLENNIALS:
INCLUSION MATTERS

Infinite diversity in infinite combinations...
Symbolizing the elements that create truth and beauty.

COMMANDER SPOCK, *STAR TREK*

I asked Andrew Stoker, a twenty-three-year-old working at an investment research firm, about the American Dream and what he thought of the traditional summary of it. These are key elements from his response: "'Prosperity through hard work' holds true ... [while] younger people are bringing some implicit interpretations behind 'hard work' that may not have existed—'hard work' is something I find interesting, enjoy, and am good at, etc. Very different interpretation of the same idea. And one more specific point that stood out was home ownership. This has probably seen a huge change. At least personally, I see myself renting for a very long time, likely with city changes included. Home ownership seems to restrict freedom, and I think more people are keying into freedom (in the sense of having flexibility) as a key part of a great life ... Perhaps the American Dream overall is becoming more experiential vs. tangible. It seems to be more about goals for having done xyz, studied xyz, or lived in xyz places instead of having certain things like a house, car, etc."

Stoker and his friends are out there with ideas, opinions, energy, and different perspectives, looking at the world with digitally-enhanced lenses, and often more inclusive approaches. I chat quite often with Stoker and his colleagues to understand more about how their energy is driving, well-aligned with, or dovetailing with Future-of-Work developments.

There is much to gain from better understanding the world we are transitioning to, which differs in many ways from the environments many of us are familiar with. Labels and laments, whomever they are said about or to, are not conducive to understanding or progress. We can all advance more smoothly and more comprehensively together. There is much benefit to bidirectional exchanges and sharing of technical expertise and experience, especially the subtle nuances of each. So, the more that different generations and all types of diverse people and perspectives come together with a mindset of inclusion and integration, the better off we will be and the more progress we will all make.

Techno-Naturals

I frequently cite Millennials as key drivers of the Future of Work, second only to technology. This is not about anyone being held responsible for instigating disruption; most of the changes have been in process for years anyway. It is more about capturing the essence of the energy that helps move the ball forward in logical ways, according to the possibilities that the new technology affords us all.

I will not debate whether Millennials (1980–1995) are acting differently from any other generation at the same ages. Generation Xers (1965–1979) were labeled the "Slacker Generation" when they were younger, just as Millennials are now often lamented as having a "poor work ethic." There are many other similarities to be made with Gen-Xers or Baby Boomers (1946–1964).[35] However, what I do observe as circumstantially different is that the younger worker cadre is the first generational group to have come into the workforce enabled by pervasive and powerful technology. Not only that, many of the digital elements were first encountered and absorbed as kids, often understood intuitively early on and later explored with the unrefined and leisure-rich exuberance of youth.

For this generation, technology often plays less of an adjunct role, supplying new and useful tools, as it is more persistently and naturally incorporated into the ongoing process of daily living. Of course, Generation Z (1996–2010) certainly is similarly facile with technology, and there are many others who have adapted quickly and almost seamlessly as capabilities and devices have been introduced and become more sophisticated. However, Millennials are currently the main body of the workforce whose world was digitally-imbued from the start. Sometimes the digital realm is an almost seamless extension of themselves, where the edges of real and virtual may not be clearly defined or controlled. They have the advantage of almost frictionless technology adoption, easily embracing powerful and versatile embedded tools and integrated solutions.

At the same time, while technology has been easing many work-related constraints, permitting new flexibility in working hours and locations especially, the modifications thus far are just a fraction of what is actually possible. Therefore, many people have seen the current developments as just the beginning of major revisions of work criteria and models. Since the employment equation has barely evolved along with society over the decades, Millennials are simply one of the visible and vocal groups bringing attention and making moves to contemporize out-of-date parameters and procedures.

Me-We-Millennials

Millennials have mostly come into the workforce just before, during, or in the aftermath of the Great Recession. A very different slate of starting-job opportunities and career trajectories—often unclear and/or networked pathways—awaited them. Full-time jobs were in short supply, much less ones that could offer long-term financial stability.

This has been the first generation to be presented with the actuality of a new, more diversified, fragmented, and constantly evolving workplace. They are the ones faced with accepting the more fluid and less stable financial- and career-related circumstances as their fundamental employment reality while they build their early careers. At the same time, many of the newcomers to the labor market were deeply affected by the way they saw older generations being treated by their employers despite long years of dedicated service.

Under these circumstances, it is understandable for employee commitment to an organization to have been impacted, with the assumption or fear of the same lack of reciprocity. It makes sense then for Millennial workers to need convincing that a company will show them loyalty or that they might want to see quick career progression as a way for a company to demonstrate its commitment to employee development and realization of their potential.

With greater economic and employment uncertainty and instability, never mind fewer prospective material rewards to accumulate, many look at work differently in terms of defining their future and determining their motivation. Hard work coupled with enjoyment and freedom is a critical part of a "great life," as Stoker noted. Therefore, if there is an alternative employment possibility that allows someone to connect with a company through shared values, a prospective hire may gravitate to this opportunity where a new employer/employee relationship, built on trust, can be envisaged. The person may well believe that this kind of relationship will better safeguard their potential and future prospects—or at least result in transparency about what the prospects really are so that they can manage them accordingly.

There is more in chapter 10 about the different context of generational groups, as well as about considering one's own context or lens and how to share assumptions and set common parameters to frame a discussion effectively. Whether there are real differences between the generations or not, the perception of differences is real and is causing resentment and misunderstanding and preventing the embracing of progress in the most productive and effective ways possible. Whatever your perspective or the perspectives of your colleagues—the way forward is *not* "us versus them." It's not about what "I" want. It's about looking beyond tone, manner, style, and more to understand what makes sense—to bring everyone along and create a viable comfortable and productive work environment.

My overarching perspective is that opinions are not facts and that there are few "right" ways of doing things—whether new or old. We have discovered that there are more-productive and less-productive ways of working and that increasing engagement will lead to greater working effectiveness *and well-being*. With more information and understanding—and greater choice to work in different ways— we can all consider new approaches and work profiles.

> "I believe that work should be one of the most fun things you do. It should excite you, it should drive you to explore more, and it should add to your being, not subtract from it. I absolutely abhor the term 'Thank God it's Friday!' Almost as bad are 'hump day!' and 'I hate Mondays.' We are a society that lives for the weekend. We are moving away from this, but yet I still worry that we spend much of our waking time longing for a time we are not in work, instead of longing to work."
>
> *Tucker Coburn, a Millennial Cornell sophomore,*
> *reflecting on "traditional" attitudes to work and*
> *aspirations for his future work environment.*

Do you have a Millennial mindset? How far has your thinking evolved to Future-of-Work ways of thinking? Which of these statements do you agree with?

- "Hard work" comprises corporate and noncorporate work, however many hours of the week each consumes.

- "Hard work" is something I enjoy.

- "Hard work" is something I have/had to suffer, especially in the early days of my career.

- Gratitude is free and can be generously given.

- Gratitude should be given in response to something worthwhile.

- Effort expended per hour of work matters, more than hours worked.

- Sometimes I work less than forty hours a week, but I am very effective during my working hours and care deeply about my work.

- If I don't work at least fifty hours a week, I feel guilty, like I have been slacking.

- I find it hard to deal with the lack of a defined workday as work and leisure activities are increasingly blended.

- I enjoy the new integration of work and other activities, leading to a more blended life, and my colleagues know the whole of who "I" am.

- Work is about finding my strengths and enjoying putting my heart into it.

- Work is about struggle and effort, and "life" begins after the workday ends.

- "Lifetime employment" means having a job for life.

- "Lifetime employment" means having to work all your life.[36]

- Freedom is not being tied to any one job or location.

- Freedom is earning enough to be able to leave if my boss is objectionable.

- Choice is being able to change working hours for specific needs/ occasions.

- Choice is being able to decide to resign from my job.

- Choice is being able to develop my own personalized work profile.

- Being risk-averse means not wanting to be beholden to a single corporation or being burdened by monthly mortgage payments.

- Being risk-averse means not changing jobs before accepting another offer.

- I perform best when I am happy at work.

- Happiness is not an emotion I associate with work.

- Working to my strengths or being focused on my passion can result in the highest productivity.

Any and all of these views and ideas can be ascribed to anyone, young or old, with many years in the workforce or a few. Many may be or at least sound like new thoughts or possibilities. Some might have only recently been expressed or are now supported by new data such as:

- Employee "happiness" (with its close association to engagement)—now a corporate objective at some companies—results in higher productivity and lower costs.

- Shared experiences from diverse perspectives lead to optimal decision-making.

We now all have a greater range of working choices, which some Millennials may find easier to explore than others, experimenting with new models and ideas, simply because they have fewer established routines. Research shows that habits are difficult to change,[37] and since change requires thought and effort, this can be challenging or uncomfortable.

That said, over the past decades, millions have been working similar fixed models, even though we are now much more aware that each individual has a very different combination of life situation, working style, noncorporate obligations, activities, needs, and desires. Embracing progress means contemplating the newly available choices that the Future of Work is bringing and finding a work model, schedule, and setup that works for each one of your workers, whoever they are, whatever their age, and whatever generation, race, gender, or other group they may be part of or identify with.

"Normally, I encourage beards, but that's not what I call a 'Millennial' beard."

Embracing Inclusion

Millennials are slated to make up around 50 percent of the global workforce by 2020[38] and some estimate they could be 75 percent of the U.S. workforce by 2030 (depending on how many Boomers retire). They are the most racially diverse generation yet, only 55.8 percent white, versus the thirty-five-to-fifty-four-year-old group (Generation X and the tail end of the Boomers), which is 61.5 percent white.[39] Millennials also currently have the lowest engagement levels at work at only 29 percent and only 50 percent plan to be with their current company in a year's time[40].

As always, younger workers are the current and future engine of growth and success. There just happen to be more Millennials than any other living generation[41], so their visibility, influence, and importance has swelled in tandem. Furthermore, with a greater diversity of perspectives, broad access to information, an easy approach to technology, and a typical attitude of youth—eg, this *is* broke, so let's fix it!—millions of Millennials are proactively embracing new ways of working. They are also showing the benefits that can accrue as they engage in the process and their work. This is creating a strategic imperative, partly through their sheer numbers.

Millennials make up the critical new and vibrant energy of your future workforce, so attracting, engaging, and retaining them is, or soon might warrant being, a priority. At the same time, every generation has an enormous amount to contribute, and inputs from everyone are valid and worthwhile to include. Baby Boomers obviously have great experience that can be leveraged in general and dedicated ways, and members of Generation X are the bulk of the current leadership and will thrive in more accommodating circumstances. To be successful in the Future-of-Work environment, it is important to respect and respond to *all* your workers.

For example, the different perspectives about technology across your workforce can be extremely useful when considering your company's digital transformation possibilities. Consider gathering a group that includes those with years of experience together with those with years of technology usage of different types, assembled with other nonadjacent disciplines, crossing functions and departments, as well as broadly inclusive of gender, race, age, and background. This will give you a compelling and diverse spectrum of viewpoints and ideas to brainstorm and envision the future direction and strategy of your company.

Different people can be engaged, stimulated creatively, and motivated in different ways. In chapter 8, I will shed more light on how to do this across your workforce. In chapter 10, I will suggest how to dismantle or smooth over challenging intergenerational conversations and attitudes in order to create the most effective working environments—virtual and physical—for your organization.

We are all individuals, first and foremost, and *then* part of other identifying groups and communities that embrace generation, race, gender, and many other dimensions. The essential point to understand is that an open and inclusive approach and policies are perhaps the most important factors for success in the Future of Work. Then you can embrace progress in a way that encompasses new ideas, ways of working, and running your business and enables comfortable integration across the workforce and the broader corporate ecosystem.

Chapter 3 Takeaways

- **First Principles**: Reflect on the fundamental premises of talent management, with an approach that encompasses comprehension and inclusion of an extensive cross section of viewpoints and mindsets. It is helpful to take time to understand the reasons behind different attitudes, tones, and styles. Consider open and embracing manners and methods to support a harmonious and productive workforce that encompasses the broadest variety of people, perspectives, and ways of thinking and working.

- **Priorities**:

  □ Engagement—Motivating and nurturing the potential of all your talent—whatever their age, generation, gender, race, or other possible defining group—is critical for your company's success. Diverse groups likely respond to a variety of methods to motivate them. Surveying your workers will surface their preferences and allow you to develop a range of means to connect them better with the company, their colleagues, and their work in an inclusive way.

▫ Personalization—Technological advances enable different ways of working, encompassing a diversity of individual needs and preferences. Survey data from employees can be leveraged to tailor personalized benefits that are offered to all.

▫ Integration—A diverse and inclusive approach to team building can help connect the individuals and teams that comprise your workforce. This approach is also effective across divisions and departments, allowing the integrated responsiveness that your company will leverage to thrive in the faster-paced marketplace.

▫ Choice—Customizable applications and approaches can permit your company to progress quickly beyond blanket approaches and policies, giving individuals choices that will make them more comfortable and able to perform better.

• **Evaluation**:

▫ Are the inputs of a broad array of technically-savvy employees solicited when considering new applications?

▫ To what extent is expertise valued over or on par with years of experience in assigning authority or allocating responsibility on a project?

▫ How much is a diversity of opinion really welcomed and recognized at your company—overall and in specific departments?

▫ How open are teams to other colleagues' ideas and viewpoints?

- □ How open are executives to experimenting with new approaches, including more flexible ways of working?

- □ How well is cross-generational communication encouraged and supported?

- □ How diverse is the age range of those developing strategic plans, including incorporation of technology internally and customer-facing initiatives such as online and mobile retail and service applications?

- **Metrics**: Increase in diversity can be monitored—by age, gender, race, etc.—with regard to the composition of teams, departments, and divisions working on all types of projects across the company. For example, the increase in number of initiatives that support different types of inclusive dialog and understanding might be tracked. For intergenerational communication, this might involve measuring an increase in the number of cross-generational mentoring pairs, as well as numbers of participants and length of participation in such programs. In addition, the diversity of leadership can be monitored; with respect to generations, examples of metrics include the percentage increase in the number of younger recruits in leadership-development programs, the increase in the number of younger employees advancing to senior positions, and the increase in diversity of senior executive committee members. Furthermore, gauging workers' responses to inclusion initiatives is important to measure to confirm they are effective.

CHAPTER 4

THE NEW RULES OF ENGAGEMENT, CULTURE FIRST

What salary would you like us to pay you?

Gavin McGarry is the CEO of Jumpwire Media, a fast-growing social media agency. He has a young workforce and, paying competitive salaries, he wants to hire the best talent he can and keep them as long as possible. He has developed some innovative ways to attract and keep his employees, based on simple premises—show them respect and value their contributions.

How does he do that? Incoming employees at Jumpwire are asked to *propose their own salary*. They are directed to specific public websites to find equivalent and adjacent jobs with market pricing for compensation. They are then given the opportunity to self-assess how much to be paid comparing demand- and value-based salaries elsewhere appropriate for their particular skills and experiences. They may want to pitch being paid at the top of the relevant salary range. If so, they are asked to substantiate their reasons. If agreed to, they then need to perform at the level appropriate with their salary.

The concept is compelling. Offering choice is powerful. What better way to immediately demonstrate your company's belief in, and respect for, new employees than to allow them to tell you how much they think they are worth and, with reasonable justification, agreeing to it? Promotion is treated the same way—when workers believe they are qualified for higher pay and a new title, it is up to them to propose the level and present their qualifications for it (again looking to third-party sources for appropriate benchmarking data). McGarry also wants employees to suggest the clients they would love to do projects for and then helps them become the sales lead for that client—who better than someone who is already a passionate fan and advocate? Simple, creative, and effective solutions enable Jumpwire Media to attract and engage some great employees.

With much corporate attention currently focused on improving productivity through engagement, let's understand what engagement is and what it is not. It is *not* the same as "employee satisfaction." It is *related* to satisfaction and happiness, but there are two important additional components—dedication and exertion. According to ADP's Research Institute, "Employee engagement is a measurement of an employee's *emotional commitment* to an organization; it takes into account the amount of *discretionary effort* an employee expends on behalf of the organization."[42]

Corporations are recognizing that the low-engagement and con-sequent low and declining productivity levels are not going to afford them important strategic advantage in the increasingly competitive and rapidly-moving marketplace. Monetary compensation, power, and status—such as salary, bonus, title, or a corner office—have historically been key levers used to incentivize people. However, other means are now better understood to stimulate interest and effort and are being broadly explored and tested, demonstrating compelling results.

Forward-thinking senior executives now have the intention to change the employment equation to increase employees' connection with their company and the meaning they find in their work, leading to improved performance and reversing declining job tenure. Many of these talent strategies and tactics have little or no relationship to money, incur nominal or no costs, and can be powerful motivators.

One example is simply showing respect for each worker as an individual allowing choices he or she never had before, so that trust can develop, permitting a reciprocal relationship to build. In addition, more relevant and specific ways of recognizing individual employees' contributions and interests are being investigated, often uncovered through surveys and then tested for practical relevance. Some strategies require thought and careful attention to execute successfully, with significant and increasingly important effect as new work-related ideas become mainstream.

Connect with Meaning

Emotional connection has never been in the standard business lexicon before. Emotions were typically left, or repressed, at the office door, as they were not welcomed within. A "business relationship" was equated with less expressive, colder, and more perfunctory communications. In the same vein, you clocked in and you checked out. You didn't try to participate as a fully-functioning human being. That was for after work. Your life "happened" before and after the workday—hence the coining of the symbolically incongruent term "**work-life balance**," which aptly captures the separation of, and conflict between, the two.

WHAT ABOUT THE MONEY?

Money is still important, don't get me wrong. However, there are many other levers, including many less expensive ones, that you can pull, which—in combination—can have more impact.

How else does the Future of Work affect compensation for your workers? It doesn't have to impact it at all. For example, workplace flexibility is not a benefit. It is a more effective way of working, so that your workers can each perform at or closer to their best, aligned with their optimal working profile as far as possible. So someone's salary is not altered if their total hours worked remains the same, while improved productivity is expected from implementing thoughtful Future-of-Work-related changes.

Nonetheless, an important aspect of the overall Future-of-Work environment involves focusing on the achievement of KPIs, project milestones, and overall results. This emphasis helps move people away from concentrating on time spent in the office and face-to-face meetings, as more workers perform their daily tasks in a variety of places. So, if your company's compensation structure is not yet outcome-focused, modification will better support your transition and help shift managers' attention in line with your new workplace strategies and policies.

There may also be some amendments as your workforce composition changes. If independent contractor numbers rise versus employees, the compensation breakdown weighting will shift, based on different payment structures—with a decrease in those receiving salaries plus benefits as compensation in different forms, to more people getting a combined total-project fee. The total amounts paid out may stay the same or change looking at on-demand, targeted needs.

Work was something to be endured or survived, not enjoyed. Work was associated with struggle and effort,[43] and a paycheck was the hard-earned "compensation." The use of this word itself is telling in that it is defined not only as "wages or salary paid by an employer to an employee" but also as "something that counterbalances or makes up for an undesirable or unwelcome state of affairs."[44] You were paid to put up with work. Indeed, at the start of my own career, I distinctly remember thinking that if people really enjoyed what they did, they probably were not being paid for it. Work and enjoyment did not "naturally" go together.

On the brighter side, as part of the greater employment equation, the almighty patriarchal corporations and factories were assumed to look after their employees for life. Many of them did "take care" of their workers from the beginning to the end of their careers, to the limited extent of what "care" encompassed at that time. However, technological advances, economic cycles, corporate short-termism, and the demise of labor unions have been contributing factors in the dismantling of these employer/employee relationships over the past few decades. The sense of belonging, trust, and security, as well as the associated dependence that came along with it, has dissipated, too, often leaving employees feeling bereft, like dispensable assets, and concerned about their future.

Both in parallel and partly resulting from this, the rising popularity of such concepts as social responsibility in business and conscious capitalism over the last decade is evidence that many people are seeking to find meaning in their professional as well as their personal lives. Purpose was something previously pursued separately from, and outside of, corporate activities. However, rather than survive grueling decades of meaningless toil and much later hope to cash in on diminished retirement benefits (whenever retirement might finally be possible), many people now want work to mean more than just a paycheck.

Millennials especially, disaffected in the aftermath of the Great Recession, have been looking for more from their work, recognizing the changing landscape and their likely reduced potential for material reward in an uncertain and lower-growth economic climate. They are actively seeking new dimensions that can add depth and connection to their working experience and contribution, assessing organizations for alignment with their own values or purpose before they will consider working there.[45]

This is important from employers' perspectives as well, since studies demonstrate that employees who feel distant and disconnected from their work do not perform as well as those who are aligned with the mission, and even purpose, of the organization they work for.[46] They ask themselves, "Why should I work here? Will anyone care about me or my contribution? Why should I stay here?"

In addition to low productivity and increasing turnover rates, higher-than-normal absenteeism (more than four days per employee per year on average[47]) can be a good indicator of corporate discontent and disconnect as employees who are not engaged also actively avoid their workplace. How involved are all your employees? Are some departments and divisions doing better than others? Are you measuring engagement levels and trying to ascertain causes as well as points of leverage? How will you differentiate your company from others to attract the talent you need going forward?

Furthermore, there is greater understanding now about those who turn up for work but are not "there" mentally and not working at full productivity. This is called "presenteeism," and it has been estimated to be far costlier to organizations than absenteeism, with a full fifty-seven and a half annual workdays squandered by employees who are not engaged in or paying much attention to their tasks.[48] There are multiple visible and latent manifestations of presenteeism—fewer innovative ideas generated, suboptimal strategies proposed, and plans poorly executed. Have you thought about how much value is not realized at your company because employees are not well-aligned with your mission or are not assigned to projects that excite or even interest them?

Concentrate on Culture

Recognizing and adding a more significant, and deeper, expression of intent is a distinctly new orientation for most corporations in the for-profit realm. Revenue and output growth were previously almost the sole objectives of companies, and their achievement was the definition of success. A secure future and increased wages for the workers were the associated benefits. Period. Now, the company's and employees' contributions to a non revenue-focused greater goal can be critical components of the overall definition of achievement for a company's employees, stakeholders, and extended corporate community.

Culture within a corporation is the sum of the attitudes, values, beliefs, and behaviors that distinguishes that company, and the collection of people who work there, from another. Everything radiates out from the central cultural core, which expresses the mindset, dictates the actions, influences the policies, and determines the environment of the organization, as well as engages the talent—internal and external—who are aligned with it.

The benefits are compounding for those businesses with a strong, pervasive, and coherent company culture. They are able to attract new hires who are similarly-oriented, reinforcing the culture as they join, as well as promote cohesive connection among employees and augment their experience and engagement, loyalty, and commitment to the company.[49] If your company has not already identified and clearly defined your corporate culture, it is increasingly important to do so. Once you do, you will be able to fully engage and retain those people who are aligned with it.

Corporate culture has many layers and manifestations, but fundamentally it is about articulating the values, purpose, and/or mission of the company, and these then determine how everything else is handled. There are many ways you can approach how you express your organizational culture. In order to determine core values and purpose, an inclusive and productive approach is to ask some or all employees to highlight key values they do or would like to associate with your company and see where there is the most overlap and agreement.

In addition, you can observe and describe the traits and values of current employees who appear to personify the desired culture and thereby help define and refine particular aspects. Certain key people can also be identified as those the firm really wants to keep, to confirm they are closely-aligned with the values being prioritized and emphasized. You want them to feel comfortable and be able to perform at the highest levels within your corporate environment. The core values are also then in accordance with the kind of people the company wants to retain and attract going forward.

Once defined and articulated in writing, the cultural components are then best communicated widely, incorporating clear and consistent messages. Over time, the cultural tenets become pervasive, embraced by your workforce, and shared externally with customers, clients, and contractors. The tenets are also conveyed around the periphery of your company's ecosystem and as part of outreach with recruiters and in all hiring conversations. A good cultural fit is critical for successful talent-growth strategies.

At Jumpwire Media, as prospects convert to employees, the values of respect and transparency are clearly conveyed in the approach McGarry has developed towards salary-setting. He reinforces the message of respect in seeking to identify and build upon employees' passions, which also helps employees enjoy and connect more deeply and engage with their work. McGarry is also very open and upfront about the possibility of employees' short tenure. While hoping to postpone departures by acknowledging retention challenges, he hopes to promote extended engagement by aligning with and feeding employees' own strengths and interests.

In the new, less authoritarian corporate environments, shared values, purpose, and vision provide a guiding framework and direction and assist the continued and consistent pursuit of company objectives. Managers are able to support employees with a different approach to oversight, so improved creativity, productivity, and associated outcomes can resonate—from workplace to marketplace. Where appropriate, purpose is being incorporated into the "corporate DNA." Acknowledgment and encouragement of a deeper connection to additional, less directly profit-driven corporate objectives are key new components in employee attraction, engagement, and retention strategies, which instead indirectly support profit-focused objectives.

Embracing Respect, Reciprocity, and Recognition

Values like respect and trust are increasingly prioritized by employees, and they go to the heart of being recognized as individuals and given more autonomy. Workers respond positively to the personalized attention they receive and respect they feel they are getting as their strengths and situations, as well as their contributions, are acknowledged. In fact, 61 percent of employees whose supervisor focused on their strengths were engaged (almost twice the average U.S. worker-engagement level).[50] In the same way, McGarry's incoming employees at Jumpwire Media understand their value is recognized on a personal level and their specific passions are surfaced and celebrated. Very different relationships can grow up between management and employees, based on trust, which become all the more critical for engagement and focused attention on tasks during uncertain and evolving times.

"I am haunted by the thought that the workers
may be unhappy."

Reciprocity is becoming a common characterisitic, changing compensation-based relationships and interactions in the workplace, and manifesting an increasingly-balanced dynamic between employer and employees as the talent agenda rises in priority. This is all the more important when the faster pace of marketplace developments requires new agility and adaptability from an organization *and* its workers. Employees are also being given more choices and the ability to adapt their own workday, to suit both the needs of the business and themselves, with a similarly-balanced approach.

Employers benefit by recognizing that their employees have different life circumstances, obligations, and activities, whether related to kids, elderly parents, marathon running, or any other hobby or interest. Accommodations are able to reduce stress and distraction from non-work-related factors. Understanding the individual and customizing work styles is often coordinated with a shift to more outcome-based metrics to shift the emphasis to work results rather than being concerned with where or how it gets done. Then, in-person meetings can start to be scheduled with specific purpose in mind instead of out of habit. This also supports the transition to having a greater prevalence of distributed workers—those workers who are not located in corporate offices but may be working from other locations, including their homes, all or some of the time.

The characteristics of leadership are changing alongside cultural elements and working models, with empathy prioritized. For leaders to engage their workers, they start by learning about and understanding who their workers are and what their choices might be and implement relevant strategies further down and throughout the organization. Management methodologies are being redesigned to incorporate the strengths and working styles of workers to leverage their full contribution potential. Adding data such as "works best at night" or "most effective when working from home a couple days a week" to an employee's working profile—the outline of a person's combination of work tasks, style, model, and hours—can help customize an individual's schedule and environment to optimize productivity.

Communicating with managers and involving them in any changes early on is important, as they will be essential to the success of any necessary modifications to the workforce dynamics. Managers are the ones in the operational trenches, on the front line of motivating workers, offering the choices, and implementing the personalized schedules. So, they need to understand and buy into why a particular change is going to be good for them, their team, and their department. The effort and time required to implement the transformation effectively can be quite substantial. However, if the managers are on board with it, and are encouraged to offer suggestions and become involved in the planning as well as the implementation, the process will go more smoothly and will almost certainly, ultimately, be more fruitful.

The core premises of employee engagement are that employees will do their best work at an organization where they are aligned with the company values, understand and can focus on their strengths, and feel comfortable with their colleagues. A first step is, therefore, to create a framework that helps workers better connect with their work, colleagues, and company. This includes assisting employees in discovering what it is that they do best or love most about their work.

Once that has been uncovered, then you can enable them to do more of it in the optimal setting possible—depending on who they are, how and where they work best, and what kind of work it is—also considering whomever they are teamed up with and whatever tools they might need. This includes providing different environments, at the office and elsewhere, that are consistent with the company culture and the tools, as well as the technical and social support that the employees will need, whether doing team work or in times of solitary concentration.

Tailored benefits are the last piece of the puzzle and will provide the other elements of well-being support—in terms of emotional, health, and other sustenance—to create the optimal ongoing experience for an employee. However, this will not be a static environment and will be evolving, and therefore regular reevaluation is appropriate to ensure that support is appropriate and sufficient over time.

The framework is provided with monitoring tools (for individuals and managers) and an ongoing review process, so relevant feedback can be shared on a timely basis to sustain project quality and progress. Recognition of accomplishments can be shared individually, with the relevant team or department, or at the organizational level, and can be easily tailored to an employee and a specific situation.

This attention and recognition can generate significant goodwill, motivating the employee to engage fully in the next task in the hope of achieving a similar response. Rewards for major accomplishments are also possible in all these situations. It is advisable to find out what recognition and reactions your specific employees prefer, using employee surveys. Then your efforts can solicit the desired response and future activity from your employees.

Since the end game for all these changes is increased productivity and greater corporate strength and success, the use of relevant metrics is essential throughout the process; first to understand the starting point, and then—as initiatives are trialed and rolled out—to discover what is working best with whom, where to focus effectively, and where and what refinements are appropriate.

Engaging *Your* Workforce

What about *your* specific company? What can you do to engage each of your workers better? Has your company made some adaptations to customize employee schedules or personalize benefits, but you still haven't seen all the positive reactions you were expecting? Have you found out what your workforce really wants?

The very concept of work as a struggle and a commonly thankless effort is receiving an inspiring rewrite, as people start to follow their passions, really engage in their work, as well as accommodate their non-corporate obligations and other activities. Now is the chance to celebrate that, and every employee, yourself included, can have the chance to both enjoy the work and perform at the highest levels. The key is first to understand and articulate your company's culture and then focus on employing and retaining those who fit into the company ethos intuitively, inherently, or explicitly. Engaged employees feel a profound connection to their company and may work with passion.

What are the best practices? As mentioned earlier, there aren't any yet. For the moment, every set of circumstances, every combination of workers and their specific roles, needs, locations, and company is unique, with some basic criteria to follow and areas to focus on. This is why taking a first-principles approach is particularly valid. The process is not complicated but is best treated with thought and attention, and making this happen for every employee in your organization obviously takes time.

An important early step is to survey your employees to find out what is important to them relevant to core engagement parameters. What type of work do they enjoy the most? What are their strengths? What flexibility is each looking for that will make a difference? Who wants to work different hours, staying at the office? Who wants to work the same hours, but working from home on some weekdays? Where do employees think they need support in developing their working profile? What benefits would resonate with each of them from a list that senior management is prepared to provide—such as tailored health and wellness benefits, volunteering days, casual dress days, and more?

As your workforce—employees and contract workers—complete the survey, they also start to understand what you are trying to achieve and that you are involving them in the process. This helps communicate the transition that is ahead and the person-alized approach that is going to be introduced. This is very helpful in building energy behind your initiatives as well as willingness to support the changes, first philosophically and then practically. In addition, "the more hours each day that Americans can use their strengths to do what they do best, the less likely they are to report experiencing worry, stress, anger, sadness, or physical pain."[51]

Then, using the survey results, you can start to map out the core elements that will engage your company's workers, including who is looking for what. You can build a picture of what these components could optimally look like for your company once implemented and prioritize which might be implemented first. Creating a trial for that area in one team or department is important so that you can test how best to execute upon these aspects and use the results and further surveying of employees participating in the trial to refine the practical implementation plans before commencing a firm-wide rollout.

Whether it relates to values, purpose, scheduling, or space—or the way they think about location altogether—companies are doing many things differently to engage their workforce. Small things as well as large. Businesses have honed in on engagement, as they want their employees to be engrossed, energized, and participating actively in their tasks and the overall progress of their company.

If anyone in your company needs convincing, remind them that your external environment affects people both inside and outside the organization. Therefore, to attract good talent, you also have to be mindful of what other companies are doing, so your firm does not get left behind. Not embracing progress, especially as it relates to employee engagement, really isn't an option anymore.

Chapter 4 Takeaways

- **First Principles**: Review the fundamental elements of engagement for achieving the strongest connection of your employees with the company. The first, most critical, elements are your corporate culture and the values and any purpose articulated. Consider how trust and respect can best be nurtured among your executives and employees. Reciprocal relationships demonstrate strong bonds, so explore how these can be developed throughout your organization.

- **Priorities**:

  □ Engagement—This is a core driver for many companies pursuing Future-of-Work progress. The increased productivity that results is a veritable win-win: employees are more stimulated and interested in their work, their performance improves, and their loyalty and tenure increases, not to mention other benefits accruing to the company. Alignment of values and purpose are key ways to engage employees, as is personalization. Recognition and tailored benefits are other ways that employee engagement can be boosted.

◻ Personalization—This is a core criterion for engaging employees—recognizing them as individuals and customizing their overall work and career experience. Their trust and respect may then be gained and their strengths identified and specifically nurtured to help develop their potential and raise engagement and performance levels.

◻ Integration—Engagement efforts are most successful when the culture is pervasive and coherent throughout the organization, employees are aligned, and engagement initiatives are consistent with the culture. It takes an integrated approach to achieve this.

◻ Choice—Connected to the personalization theme, offering new choices to employees is a critical factor in enabling them to feel recognized as valued individuals, and respect results. A different relationship can build with a deeper connection between the company and an employee. Choice is a powerful motivating factor in your engagement toolbox.

- **Evaluation:**

  ◻ How well is your company's culture articulated?

  ◻ Is it clearly understood by all executives, managers, and employees?

  ◻ How is it communicated externally to customers and vendors, as well as in recruiting messages? How well are employees trusted and respected?

  ◻ How is their value demonstrated to them internally, as well as externally to customers?

- □ What kind of choices do employees have at different levels of the company hierarchy?

- □ How comfortable are they with the options they have—about their choices of focus and projects and their work schedules and location?

- □ How are employees recognized when they achieve something special?

- □ Is the executive team comfortable with the levels of absenteeism?

- □ Are turnover levels high or increasing?

- **Metrics**: Employee-engagement surveys are proliferating and may be selected for applicability to your organization. It is beneficial to review and select specific elements within those surveys, as well as adding elements that may be useful for identifying aspects that are not yet included. Consider aspects that demonstrate the external effects of increased engagement, such as customer satisfaction. Metrics for monitoring the development of an engagement program might include: percentage of managers involved in developing the engagement initiatives; and managers' satisfaction with the initiative elements, roll-out, and impact. Metrics for tracking the impact might include the percentage decrease in absenteeism, percentage decrease in "presenteeism," and employee willingness to recommend your company to others.

CHAPTER 5

LEADERSHIP: EGO AND EMPATHY

When the best leader's work is done, the people say, 'We did it ourselves.'
LAO TZU

arey Smith founded and runs Big Ass Solutions, an expanding, thousand-plus-person multinational company. He is an inspiring leader who really understands what it takes to engage his company's employees, and one of those employees introduced us so that I could learn about his empathetic and inclusive leadership approach, which is compelling and certainly far from traditional.

First, as one early indication of his approach, Smith listened to the no-nonsense feedback of their early client base of facility managers and changed the company's name from HVLS Fan Company (High

Volume Low Speed, as they started out making high-quality industrial fans). Second, Smith makes *all* decisions by consensus, clearly communicating to everyone his role relative to theirs and the value of each person's contribution to the whole business.

The name change and consensus-driven approach are symbolic of Smith's leadership style—listening carefully and highly respecting the inputs of customers and employees alike. Smith has a different and inclusive interpretation of ego, which extends far beyond himself to encompass all employees, who together are a "tribe."

Smith has been laser-focused on building the best-quality products possible, with an intention to create products that never wear out. Smith's passion for excellence is one of his greatest assets for attracting and retaining the top talent he needs in order to grow and expand the product lines and company overall. His leadership focus is also on talent and developing his people to be the best they can possibly be. Smith has purposefully established an environment where workers are inspired continually to rethink, reimagine, rework, and adapt, in order to develop and take advantage of their strengths and create new ideas to improve the products they make. Employees are most appreciative, and the company has only a 15 percent turnover rate—despite having a significant composition of sought-after, highly-skilled engineering talent and a young employee base.

Smith also makes a habit of walking around the offices and visiting employees, asking each of them, "Where do you want to be in five years? How much do you want to be earning? What do you want to be doing?" Whatever their response, he helps them develop a plan to progress toward it and get them started. Smith is profoundly thoughtful about the culture he has built, based on trust and respect, including his attitude towards his employees and the time they spend working at the company. "I am buying part of their lives," he said. "It would be selfish not to take this responsibility seriously."

Smith is an example of the emerging face of leadership. Ego is defined, at the company level, as an expression of the corporate culture and not the CEO. Leaders who embody the identity of their company can convert from "traditional," often autocratic, direction from the top—increasing employees' choices and giving them more compelling and effective guidance and leadership.

With the progressive focus on engagement, new leaders recognize and are empathetic about the needs of their employees. The flattening of the "information power pyramid," coupled with increased employee autonomy, has created a more equal and reciprocal relationship between leadership and the rest of the workforce. New-style leaders now solicit their workers' opinions in flatter, more peer-based, and more transparent operating environments. They focus on employees' strengths and actively seek to inspire and motivate them to achieve the levels of productivity that are essential to compete effectively in today's global business environment.

Shifting Identity and Choice

The "ego" of the emerging brand of leadership is not the "command and control" type of autocrat that this word has evoked in the past. Now, it's more about empathy—creating an environment based on trust and respect—in order to engage the workforce and improve *employee ego*, stimulating their self-awareness and self-worth. Ego here is also about the company's identity, the values and purpose that the leadership aligns with.

When leaders understand the identity of their company and the workers that comprise it, leading people is more about engaging and guiding them. Values echoed by the leaders of a company offer a clear and more "natural" direction for the workforce to follow in their own actions, relating to everything from daily tasks to long-term goals and career planning. When and if there are problems dealing with strategy or competition, for example—both in transition and in the future—having everyone aligned with the company's cultural identity means consensus and solutions can be reached more easily.

"Who would like to give me feedback on my
leadership qualities?"

At its core, ego in leadership is now about inclusiveness and empathetic understanding of each employee as a complete individual. It is the philosophy behind the request that workers "bring their whole selves" to work, which actually makes them more valuable to the company and more at ease themselves when they do. When communicated consistently and sincerely that each employee is a capable individual and team member, respect is generated that deepens their relationship with the company and involvement in its progress and success.

When each person's contributions are regularly recognized and supported, their opinions more valued, and decisions followed, responsibility and accountability shifts from the leader toward the employees. This more-connected, empathetic, and nurturing kind of leadership is shown to generate greater productivity as each employee recognizes his or her participation in achieving the company's goals. Transformational leaders deliberately adopt the perspective that this is proactively and purposefully transferring—not losing—choice and control to employees, as increased autonomy is a critical component for increasing engagement.[52] Smith's approach exemplifies this principle. The company's retention rate reflects employees' response to his purposefully shifting control to share the choices and decision-making with them. The resulting sense of mutual accountability among everyone at the firm also becomes a powerful bond.

Progress in leadership style will be most effective when it is consistent throughout an organization and, therefore, applies to all executives and managers, not just the chief executive at the top. It is important that any transfers of authority are understood and recognized by everyone in the company, acknowledging movement as movement along the employer-employee continuum of choice and accountability. All employees can then develop a comprehensive understanding of the new scope of their roles and responsibilities, including their more proximate relationships, the resulting flatter hierarchy, and a better sense of their contributions to and ownership of the future success of the company.

Hierarchy and Transparency

The shift of control has been experienced in many areas with the advent and widespread dissemination of information through the Internet. Previously, information equated to power, but almost universal access to data has redistributed power, with numerous consequences. A shift has also begun to occur in how leaders of individual projects are selected, with an emphasis on expertise rather than years of service. For instance, someone who is twenty-five could be the most senior person working on the development of a new mobile application. Their four years investigating, experimenting, developing, and building apps (and perhaps a decade of intense total usage) could be at least two years more than anybody else in their division. In a new and fast-evolving field, this experience differential can equate to substantially more knowledge and understanding and warrant leadership of the specific project.

A long-established, fixed, and multitiered hierarchical approach, focused on tenure and years of experience, is essentially flipped for one that heavily prioritizes relevant expertise and skill. Since the area of focus can depend on the particular project, it means that authority itself can be more fluid, and possibly the accompanying hierarchy as well—in some areas not necessarily all. The authority can then be both temporal and distributed among the leaders of prevailing projects. The scope of new leaders, therefore, is also to become more attuned to the composition of senior team members and dispersal of authority within the company, both of which might look significantly different over the course of a financial year.

Big Ass Solutions is a good example of this new type of flatter, more-fluid organization. Smith is not interested in titles and hierarchy (externally his official title is "Chief Big Ass"). Internally, he only focuses on the talent, effort, and results of each individual. However, he appreciates certain requests by employees negotiating with other companies to have titles commensurate with an equivalent external position in order to promote peer relationships. That said, the organization is not flat. There are select levels attributed to expertise, and Smith realizes the need for these limited strata to facilitate appropriate connections and interactions between increasingly dispersed employees, especially as the company expands further internationally.

The new weighting on expertise has also stimulated and supported development of relationships based on reciprocity and respect rather than an emphasis on veneration for titles or years at the company. Organizational structures are already 25 percent flatter than they were in the late 1990s.[53] Status is derived now more from an employee's intent, effort, and effective contribution—achieving progress for the company, just as at Big Ass Solutions. This is possible for any employee, even the newest or youngest one, which can be a strong motivating opportunity for them.

So, the flatter hierarchy dynamic offers opportunities to have a more reciprocal type of communication, more peer-based interaction, and exchange of information and ideas with a more equal give-and-take between workers and leaders. Executives and managers can better appreciate the benefit of progress represented by these new operating practices, as well as the strong interest in them, recognizing that rivalry for talent is only going to get tougher. Plus, the timely sharing of information and ideas can be a competitive requirement in a fast-evolving marketplace.

Greater corporate transparency both results from and promotes less-stratified corporate structures. Previously, leaders could control most of what was presented externally about their company, whether through advertising, press releases, newsletters, or otherwise. Now, social media and other applications and platforms have enabled everyone—especially customers—to voice their opinions publicly about business decisions and performance as well as the company's products and services. Therefore, leaders have had to accept that such information—good, bad, and possibly erroneous or ugly—will be shared, and often judged, and that responses will be necessary.

The accelerated customer-feedback loop and possible interactions at every stage of production or provision of a company's products or services has significantly changed the business dynamics and often the processes.[54] This involves leadership managing a very different environment—where control, secrecy, and fixed structure yield to openness, transparency, and a flexible attitude. This can be hard to adjust to and get comfortable with, especially at the speed that is sometimes necessary. If there is a corporate incident which is not met with a swift response that the public deems appropriate, then there can be a significant and negative impact on the company. Examples include Toyota's delayed reaction to accidents resulting from sticky accelerator pedals starting in 2007, and Chipotle's delayed response to E. coli-related food-poisoning incidents in several states in 2015. Both of these resulted in lingering negative impact to the company's stock price and reputation.

In addition, a consequence of the exposure of much company information dictates that the core messages, which communicate the essence of the corporate culture, values, and vision, be consistent. Any incongruence or disconnect is noticed and has the ability to cause confusion or even unease for both employees and customers. So, as leaders articulate the company values, it is very important that the same vision, phrases, and cadence be communicated clearly internally and externally. Amazon had issues in 2015 and 2016 relating to discrepancies between corporate messages and former employees' stories, which made some employees *and* customers uncomfortable.

Wider dissemination of corporate information has created the expectation of employee involvement at all levels of an organization, including participation at every stage of the process. This serves further to flatten the perception and reality of the corporate structure. The large population of **knowledge workers**—as defined by Peter Drucker in 1956—does not want to be directed. Peter Drucker cautioned that "knowledge workers have to manage themselves. They have to have autonomy."[55]

This especially applies to younger employees, who started their working careers with great access to information and much more understanding of the machinations of business than many of their predecessors and older colleagues.[56] This is part of Smith's purposeful leadership strategy in engaging all types of team members in different group decisions—they actively participate in, and own, the future successes and failures of the business.

In exploring less stratified, much flatter organizational models, different concepts are proposed that can be explored. Some ideas reject titles entirely, with each project team decided by consensus, based purely on expertise. Certain concepts have been received with mixed reactions with their perceived or actual focus on process rather than engaging employees and personalizing the work experience in a meaningful way. Therefore, it is worth thoughtfully researching the possibilities. It may be wise to consider the basic model elements that you are interested in that can be interpreted differently, applied in various ways, and adopted to degrees deemed acceptable and viable. These all depend on the circumstances specific to your company, business, and talent. What does appear to be a consistent theme is that the fixed, hierarchical "structure" itself, which holds the "building blocks" of organizational design, and the static, multi-layered immutable image it evokes, now seems almost antithetical to the progressive, more dynamic, and flexible working environment.

Leading from Within

For leaders now, the success factors include a progressive, open attitude to new ideas and processes, wherever they may come from, and the embracing of flexibility and adaptability across the organization, not supporting separate division silos. This is not from a singular, personal perspective, but from a comprehensive one, incorporating many ideas that are solicited cross-functionally. This represents a stark departure from legacy modes of operation for most companies.

Successful implementation of a consistent and thorough change of approach—rooted in, and radiating out from, the corporate culture—is not easy and requires thoughtful and dedicated execution. It is possible to adopt a new leadership style—transitioning in incremental steps, allowing for trial and error, and carefully tracking your successes and failures, while leveraging the essential characteristics of adaptability and flexibility along the way. Calculated action in the present is needed to change the way talent is empowered and guided and work is accomplished in order to move the company forward and ensure a thriving work and business future. At Big Ass Solutions, Smith tried many different performance-review systems and methodologies. In the end, he has found that an inclusive and attentive personal approach yields the best results for empowering and motivating employees to make progress and advance the company's growth and success.

One high-level question to address is how much the leadership at different levels of your company needs to adapt—what is the level of awareness of team leaders and their understanding about their team members and their adaptability? A few questions to start asking yourself and other leaders/managers include:

- How are the cultural values demonstrated daily in operating procedures and interactions?

- Are you comfortable with the skills and expertise of your teams? Are their skills being kept up-to-date?

- How well do you know the strengths and interests of individual managers and their team members?

- Where could your leaders start to delegate more—immediately and over time?

- What tools are used to give clear direction and track projects and tasks?

- Are team members able to monitor and complete tasks with nominal input/limited supervision?

- How are respect and trust towards employees best demonstrated during the workday by team leaders?

The impact of this new leadership and progress to a flatter hierarchical approach is pervasive. The effective transformation is from a fixed, highly-structured, and tightly-controlled pyramid of accountability to more of an umbrella framework that empowered employees work within on assigned projects. This is a significant change for most companies, philosophically and practically, and leads to a very different way of tracking tasks and progress for business units.

As new leadership methods are introduced, each employee's new roles and capabilities can be newly clarified and defined. Using new platforms and tools, leaders and supervisors can then monitor how each of their employees is dealing with the new responsibilities and give suitable support to those who require it initially and/or ongoing. Many managers already have a reasonable understanding of how their different team members work and the level of individual oversight they may need to work most effectively. However, executive team members and supervisors will be managing units where schedules may be newly-personalized and workers more frequently dispersed in different combinations, so new management approaches may be introduced with training to support the transition.

Relinquishing some of management's hold on daily tasks also means that goals, project milestones, and deadlines are more explicitly described to ensure everyone is clear about their responsibilities and are measured and accountable. Some people are comfortable working more independently, and others thrive in situations that emphasize teamwork. Self-awareness—each person's understanding of their own identity, working style, and role—therefore becomes more important in the new working environment. It provides valuable input for any team manager or member to optimize each worker's personal effort and contribution to the unit, team, and task at hand. Employees have different abilities and speeds of adaptation to the new circumstances, and positions may need to be modified to accommodate and align with their preferred working styles. So, the support of team leaders at all levels is important when adjusting to more customized work parameters.

In the end, the pace and ease of making progress ultimately depends on how each leader responds and adapts to changes in workforce dynamics. Leading progress through significant change can seem a daunting task, but the benefits that stand to be gained are far greater—from a healthier work environment and improved employee well-being to the consequent increased productivity and profits. Accepting and adopting these elements of progress is necessary to remain competitive these days. Smith shares the profits of his company's labor with the whole tribe to reinforce how everyone is part of its success.

Chapter 5 Takeaways

- **First Principles**: Contemplate the core elements of leadership, while acknowledging the shift in emphasis toward employees and toward leading from within the organization rather than from the top, with an empathetic approach. There is also a more inclusive and intimate sense of corporate identity, partially resulting from greater information flow and transparency, creating more balanced, reciprocal dynamics between leaders and employees. Consider how transparency of information affects executive and manager relationships with employees and how it affects customers. Reflect on the nature of interactions and relationships within the organization and how and where hierarchy assists and hinders these exchanges, associations, and dependencies.

- **Priorities**:

  ▫ Engagement—More emphasis on expertise than years of experience can be a strong motivator in engaging younger employees, enhanced by the resulting flatter corporate hierarchy that also shifts internal relationships. With the transition to giving employees more responsibility, it is important to define new roles and responsibilities clearly.

□ Personalization—With fewer titles and layers, and more peer-to-peer interaction, more intimate connections can develop throughout an organization, which can increase engagement and loyalty and reduce turnover.

□ Integration—Greater transparency results from increased access to and sharing of information. More cross-functional teams and projects flatten the hierarchy and enhance greater peer-based communication and sharing of ideas, increasing the company's ability to be responsive and agile.

□ Choice—The offering of more options to workers by leaders is recognized as a shift along the employer/employee continuum of accountability towards employees—a key characteristic of the Future-of-Work environment in general.

- **Evaluation**:

  □ How empathetic is the leadership of your company?

  □ How many strategic decisions include lower-level managers?

  □ How many levels of hierarchy does your company have? Has that decreased over the last three years?

  □ Do your employees have more options regarding their work format or profile than three years ago?

  □ How much information about company progress and results is shared openly with employees?

  □ How are technology-focused projects managed, and by whom?

  □ How much are employees involved in departmental decision-making?

◻ To what degree are employees' opinions solicited and incorporated?

◻ How many cross-functional teams are there working on projects?

• **Metrics**: Examples include: Increase in the number of project decisions delegated to lower-level managers or team members; increase in percentage of employees included in company-wide decisions; increase of work-related options offered to employees to select from when developing their personalized working profiles; increase in the number of workers taking advantage of the broader range of work options; increase in training support for managers to assist their team members in developing new work scenarios.

CHAPTER 6

PRODUCTIVITY, PERFORMANCE, AND PERSONALIZATION

The ladder of success is best climbed by stepping on the rungs of opportunity.

AYN RAND

A record 658 million vacation days went unused by U.S. workers in 2015. This was up from 429 million unused vacation days in 2014, an increase of more than 50 percent. For the first time ever, the majority (55 percent) of Americans did not take all their vacation days. Why? Mostly, they didn't feel supported,[57] and likely their bosses didn't take all their vacation, on up the chain to the leader at the top. Leaders set the example.

What have unused vacation days got to do with progress and productivity? Everything. If your employees are going to do their best work for you, they need to have the energy and focus, never mind the intention, to do it. Burnout undermines performance, and thence productivity, so such conditions are important to change as part of your overall plan for progress. The reality is that the impetus to galvanize your company—to make the significant investment of time, effort, and energy to transition to the Future-of-Work environment—is generated in great part by a desire to improve productivity and performance. The powerful, matching benefit is that the changes forecast will also improve the well-being of your employees.

First, most immediately, you want to counter existing hiring or retention issues (possibly Millennial-related?), or you are concerned about potential ones. Second, you are keen to ensure that your company is not at a strategic disadvantage and can be responsive to marketplace disruption and developments. Third, you recognize that your talent is critical to your future, and you want to engage them through personalization in positive ways *and* increase the contributions of each to the company's bottom line. That is to say, you are looking to improve employees' individual performances and participation resulting in higher personal productivity and corporate profit as a consequence.

Fourth and last, running in parallel with any transformation or adaptations that are embarked upon, you want to ensure that everything is measurable and measured and that you can track the very specific impact on overall productivity and individual performance of all the adjustments made. It will therefore be important to set a baseline at the beginning, before applying appropriate methods and utilizing relevant metrics. These will also enable you to monitor trials, make refinements as test results and feedback are received—as well as surface evidence and confirm the benefits of modification plans executed.

Pursuing Productivity

In a competitive marketplace—whether local, regional, national, or international—improving productivity is essential, especially in view of the prevailing low and declining levels. Increasing productivity is core to the transformation to the Future-of-Work environment, which brings the focus upon talent and technology. Your talent is the energy and creative brains of your company. Therefore, the emphasis of efforts is to engage them, personalize their work and career experiences, and give them more choices which will then translate into gains in productivity. And technology, as explained earlier, is the powerful driver, enabler, supporter, and overall integrator of new talent-focused and operational changes that enhance communications, interactions, processes, and even business models.

Engagement is the most important factor in pursuing productivity improvements. In Gallup's 2013 analysis of 1.4 million employees, teams in the top 25 percent of employee engagement outperformed the bottom 25 percent by 21 percent in productivity and 22 percent in profitability. In addition, highly-engaged organizations have experienced double the success rate of less engaged ones. [58]

Nonetheless, for all the focus on corporate revenues, earnings, and growth, defining and calculating productivity has actually been a moving target for decades. Those doing "knowledge work" or non-routine cognitive work are an increasing portion of the American labor force and made up a full 40 percent of the U.S. economy in March 2016.[59] However, knowledge work mostly creates intangible results that are extremely varied in nature, and "output per worker" as a metric is typically not applicable. As a result, there remains much ongoing research, debate, and emerging possible solutions as to how and what to measure relating to knowledge-worker productivity.

Still, plans for transformation to the Future-of-Work environment certainly need to include appropriate metrics to track and measure the effects and benefits of the adaptations. Moreover, in certain areas, since the process may take some time, the ongoing monitoring is important as the rollout is executed and refinements are made. Short-, medium-, and long-term milestones are important to include as circumstances continue to evolve, and adjustments will likely be made to newly-implemented situations in accommodation.

A myriad of metrics already exist to evaluate productivity. It is critical to ensure that the metrics you are using for measurement do actually correlate with the elements you want to understand, track for trending purposes, and be able to project forward. Many companies do not evaluate what factors are, in fact, the important ones to measure for their particular business and company. The Balanced Scorecard and the Baldrige Excellence Framework,[60] both of which take a broad and systematic approach, are two pretty comprehensive solutions that have been widely adopted. In specific areas, particular criteria may be identified as especially relevant to support and monitor productivity improvements for certain parts of your organization and business.

Especially with the impact of engagement on productivity, it is now essential to capture important *intangible* metrics as part of your overall productivity and performance calculations. New understanding about knowledge-worker productivity reveals factors that are affected by the coherent integration of human resources, facilities management, and information technology, which will be covered in chapter 8. These factors include employee sentiment about trust, autonomy, security, and social aspects, as well as workers' effort and intent. All of these factors can be measured using qualitative metrics in order to evaluate and get a comprehensive read of the holistic working environment and employees' productivity therein.

Shifting the Performance Paradigm

At the same time as productivity metrics have been evolving, so have performance reviews and methodologies been scrutinized—and these are also in the process of being revised and updated. Considering the faster marketplace developments, the traditional once-yearly timing has been too static to keep pace with market evolution. The annual review has been insufficiently frequent to track changing objectives and project outcomes in a timely manner, or to capture well-directed efforts or catch misaligned ones.

In numerous cases, performance reviews are evolving into less formal and more regular—at least quarterly, if not monthly, or possibly even daily—exchanges with employees about project-specific progress and their relative performance. Salary reviews still mostly remain once-yearly, but ratings systems are being questioned. Not only can they often foster unhealthy internal competition, but ratings are associated with significant annual cost and are subject to strong bias, which Deloitte has highlighted publicly. Major companies such as Goldman Sachs, Accenture, General Electric, Gap, Adobe, and Microsoft have reworked their reviews and/or abolished their ratings systems.[61]

In April 2015, Deloitte announced the results of a public survey they conducted to understand the efficacy of performance-management systems. They discovered that for their own organization, the whole process, company-wide, consumed around two million man-hours a year to complete. In addition, they found that 80 percent of the rating was dependent on the perspective of the person doing the rating, meaning that the results were mostly subjective. What is more, they found that their performance-management approach did *not* positively impact employee engagement *or* improve performance.[62]

"Your evaluation is based on the next
10 minutes of work. Go!"

Annual reviews are inherently backward-facing in nature. However, learnings from the past would best be utilized to the fullest to improve performance going forward. Still, there can often be a disconnect from the future needs of the company that an employee is there to help fulfill. Hence, Deloitte's updated, forward-looking emphasis became more about "fueling performance" in the future.

In addition, ongoing weekly check-ins between Deloitte's supervising managers and employees were found to offer a more proactive and productive approach, helping align an individual's performance, career growth, and evolution as well as the company's overall productivity. Career development is a critical element in worker motivation. So if you address the nurturing of your employees' potential, it will simultaneously provide additional input toward their incentivization and consequent performance.

Striking a good balance in the frequency and content of updated reviews reinforces the idea for employees that their employer is supportive and actively collaborating with them to check in and understand their progress. A supervisor has the opportunity to share beneficial feedback to enhance employees' work output *and* experience. Executed well, reviews can feel more natural and constructive—less like interrogations and more like conversations. There is a clear purpose for the discussion of helping individuals perform to the highest level—aligning well with company objectives, focusing on strengths, and identifying and reducing stress or unhappiness in the workplace—thereby boosting productivity.

Key performance indicators (KPIs), as the metrics that demonstrate how effectively your company is achieving important business objectives, are obviously useful for determining achievement. Appropriate KPIs depend on your industry and the business unit being monitored, based on relevant business goals such as customer-lifetime value, product rates of return, social-media conversion rates, service level availability and utlization, and expense levels.

However, product cycles are now iterating on a much more frequent basis,[63] as are service upgrades and revisions as the pace of innovation speeds up. It is therefore important to acknowledge that select KPIs might sometimes need updating within a period of months. For example, after developments in the marketplace, if customers or clients are no longer evaluating your product or service in the same way, certain KPIs may need to be changed. Tracking to out-of-date targets is redundant and demotivating for employees. However, it is still an adjustment for managers and employees alike, dealing with what might seem like moving targets, and thought and attention is needed from both parties to manage effectively. It is helpful to focus on what the project or company is ultimately trying to achieve, and shorter-term goals can assist transition.

Overall, an important general shift is to outcome-based performance metrics. This approach allows everyone, no matter where they are working from—and when and how—to be evaluated based on their work achievement, with a critical de-emphasis on in-person appearances. Tools for tracking results for individual employee performance may well be different for those working outside the office the majority of the time. Remote workers are best assigned their work—its definition, milestones, and deadlines—with great detail and specificity in order to ensure that expectations are set, are communicated clearly, and can be met. Similarly, performance review methodology—its formulation and inputs—optimally recognizes and is adapted for remote work locations. Specific weighting may be given to certain factors that can easily be determined at a distance, utilizing the tools at the person's disposal, with the understanding that well-supported remote working environments are critical.

A related aspect is the recognition and promotion of remote workers, which impacts their performance. When promotions arise, those employees who are mostly present in the office tend to be the ones top of mind for managers. This is only natural, since they are closer physically and interactions are in person and usually more frequent. However, if assessments are focused on results, all workers' performance can be consciously evaluated on a comparable basis, focusing on their completion of tasks as defined. Care can be taken to ensure that remote workers are judged using the same parameters as their in-office peers, depending on their achievements, if all locations are supported equally.

It can be useful to stimulate activities or other projects outside normal job functions to bring people together and very specifically including all remote workers possible. By creating opportunities for employees to participate in events outside of their job function, you can also help ensure that they are more integrated into the corporate community, as well as their managers' consciousness, no matter where they are working from.

In line with actively promoting and supporting a collaborative work environment—discussed further in chapter 8—group performance is another new area of interest for companies to understand and evaluate. Some middle schools and high schools are incorporating "group grades" for projects in certain subjects, developing appropriate teamworking skills and preparing Generation Z for this type of work format and performance framework. My son, for example, has been graded on participation and a variety of criteria to assess his contribution to the team, as well as the team's achievement. The teams are also evaluated and scored on how well their members interact with one another, all with the intention of encouraging productive collaboration.

Companies are interested in promoting, tracking, and rewarding group performance,[64] while teams in the future are as likely to be spread across continents as they are rooms. In this regard, it is important to select a coherent measurement system that is capable of taking the context of the work and workers involved into account. At the same time, dispersed individuals and teams—whether regionally, nationally, or internationally—need to have similarly strong environments to perform in if they are each going to be evaluated using appropriate (relative) metrics.

As described earlier, engaging employees to be much more productive is a whole new ballgame that has only just begun, and the rules are still being written. For once, it really *is* about taking it personally. . .

The Personalization Gap

Productivity, performance, and personalization are tightly related, making the mission to engage workers a very personal one in and of itself. Leaders at every level of the organization will address and accommodate each person in their team(s) as an individual in multiple dimensions if they are to achieve close to the levels of performance that each and every employee is capable of. As described in preceding chapters, separate and interrelated research demonstrates that people do best when: they are individually respected, they are able to pursue their purpose, they work to their strengths, their work schedule accommodates noncorporate obligations and activities, their work is recognized,[65] and they receive personalized benefits.

As discussed earlier, purpose is a critical personal motivator. People can be driven by the purpose of the company, the intrinsic value of the work they do, and/or their own personal mission. If connected to the value of the work itself, an individual will stay longer at a company and perform better. Workers with a purpose orientation have a 20 percent longer expected tenure, are 50 percent more likely to be in leadership positions, are 47 percent more likely to be promoters of their employers, and have 64 percent higher levels of fulfillment in their work.[66]

Helping people find a personal connection to their jobs is one of the best ways to stimulate the intrinsic value they feel for their work. Like most matters surrounding productivity, intrinsic value has a lot to do with company culture and hiring people who are well-aligned with the company's mission and values. This makes clear internal and external communication of these aspects critical for successful achievement of your talent-focused agenda, so that everyone is abundantly aware of the identity of the company and what you are trying to accomplish.

That said, most people have little idea about their own purpose—and may well have never associated "purpose" with a corporate job or for-profit pursuit. On a more practical level, few people have ever considered the possibility of choice and are at a loss when asked how they might optimally design their work—focusing on what they are best at, and what they enjoy most, what timing they would prefer, and where they would like to do it. StrengthsFinder is one useful tool to help employees understand and develop their strengths and what they are most interested in doing.

Implementing **workplace flexibility** successfully is a multistep and multidimensional process. For a start, a significant percentage of people do not know their optimal work style as one organizing principle—do they work best at night, in the morning, surrounded by people, with a team, or by themselves? In traditional corporate roles, there has not been much explicit call for great self-awareness or choice offered to find this out. In highly-controlled situations, given strict instructions, and working within rigid structures, there was little need and less room for any personal digressions. Personality tests—such as Myers Briggs and Harrison Assessments—can support the process to develop a working profile, helping individuals understand more about their key characteristics to provide helpful inputs for the choices to be made.

WHAT ABOUT HOURLY WORKERS?

Not all the aspects of the Future of Work that I describe in this book are necessarily applied in the same way or to the same degree for every group of employees, nonemployee workers, or type of work. This is part of what makes the Future-of-Work environment more complex to strategize and plan for. Different worker groups are impacted in different ways, depending on their roles and the prevailing control they have over their jobs, and each scenario is worth looking at and addressing specifically.

For example, certain recent technology developments in the workplace have undermined workers' situations by increasing the unpredictability of their income streams and daily schedules. In one such scenario, this is manifested by the use of sophisticated software in fast-food restaurants to be able to forecast and optimize the number of hourly workers needed to staff a particular location, almost in real-time. Workers may be alerted with just a few hours' notice and have to scramble to find childcare, if needed. Unpredictable schedules can also prevent someone from getting a second part-time job if the additional income is needed, further damaging the person's economic circumstances.

Personalization and more choices are critical for these workers and can be achieved by giving them more schedule options and longer lead-times. Working arrangements for the Future-of-Work environment are optimized when fulfilling balanced policies that are aligned with your culture and taking into account the needs of your workers.

When offered workplace flexibility, employees are put in a position to consider and develop their own optimal working profiles as their desired job outline and composition, including the work they do, their preferred schedule, and the location(s) the work is performed. Guidance and coaching are recommended for employees and managers to enable them each to create a personalized work scenario that will allow them to flourish and perform at their highest levels. This is the case for all ages and most types of jobs and employees. Younger recruits have much less working experience to draw on to evaluate their options, while older ones often had very few alternatives to consider in most of their working situations, and they can find the new range of choices confusing no matter how obvious the benefits—see chapter 10.

Another important step in the process of setting up a new personalized work environment is to help employees understand how to identify and define their preferred working hours and locations, particular working styles, life circumstances, and other obligations. Your company's support and direction for each as individuals will allow them to create the least stressful and most productive work situation for themselves, which is then coordinated with their team members to be most effective and productive for all. The integrated involvement helps to build the trust that the new, more personal and reciprocal employer/employee relationships are founded on.

The outcome of the process is that each employee will have a new personalized schedule that may then be trialed, tweaked, and transitioned to. Your employees will be much more productive—more engaged and less distracted, with much more energy, attention, and enthusiasm to apply to their business-related tasks and projects. Not only will their overall well-being improve; numerous studies have shown that they will also be more loyal, less likely to leave your company, and more likely to recommend it to others and attract the top talent you need to be successful.[67]

Recognition is another way to validate an employee and promote their continued enthusiasm and contribution level, as covered in chapter 4. The last important levers are the benefits offered by your company, which may be utilized to address the new emphasis on personalization—individually supporting your employees to stimulate their engagement and performance.

Motivating Benefits

Employee benefits and perks can certainly promote, and even improve, performance, especially when related to health. It is recognized that healthy employees are both more resilient and more productive, since they are not distracted or undermined physically or mentally by illness.[68] Consequently, there is movement toward value-based assessments of wellness instead of cost-focused ones, to acknowledge that the gains from such programs go well beyond reduced health-related costs.[69]

In the increasingly customized work world, what does each person want, and how can your company handle all the different possibilities? Conducting an employee survey is an important next step when looking to update or develop the most advantageous incentives and wellness programs. For a start, surveys help to identify what people really want instead of what others think they want. In addition, some of the things or changes actually desired are of minimal cost or effort to offer, in contrast to what may be anticipated.

Surveys have an added value in overtly asking for employees' input. Just the act of asking helps employees understand that you are trying to address their needs and requests, even if not all of them can be met, or perhaps not yet. Increased internal dialog can be very useful in gaining employees' personal insights about the company and suggestions about how it can operate better, bringing ideas from people who really know what is going on in detail and have different perspectives. Such interactions also offer an opportunity to share the challenges and trade-offs that management faces, so that employees might even participate in (re)prioritizing or in/excluding elements. They then have greater personal investment in the company overall, as well as understanding more about, and having ownership of, the choices made—even if certain decisions go against certain specific desires.

Employee feedback during the process helps ensure that the benefits are consistent with the culture and spirit of the company. A discord between the type of perks offered and the values communicated to employees is quickly understood, and coherence is necessary to support and motivate the workforce. This was clear to the CEO of the 86 Company, Malte Barnekow. He heads up an organization that is pioneering in its collaboration with top international distilleries and bartenders to create and distribute unique liquors.

Barnekow was concerned about employee retention and attraction during a critical fast-growth period, and he wanted to offer benefits that truly delivered on their desired results. He was conceptually curious about unlimited vacation and what other offerings might be appropriate for the dedicated and enthusiastic employees who call themselves a family.

As highlighted at the beginning of this chapter, 658 million vacation days went unused in 2015, a significant increase from the 429 million in 2014. This behavior is not healthy for employees. Productivity is reduced if employees do not get the rest they need to regenerate their energy and enthusiasm for their work, and the risk of heart disease and heart attacks goes up.[70] Research also shows that fourteen days of contiguous time off is needed to get the full recuperative benefit and "regather crashed resources."[71]

Barnekow reviewed the research, their employee survey results, and the variety of vacation options, ranging from unlimited to mandatory, from length to timing. With the ongoing intensity of work during their growth phase and the need for everyone to be performing at their highest levels, he was focused on the necessary restorative aspects of benefits. He and the rest of the partnership/ executive team agreed on a generous increase to fifteen paid days off for all employees in addition to the two-week winter shutdown in December. Most importantly, as part of this, one fourteen-day stretch each year (including weekends) was not mandated, but strongly recommended, and, if taken, an extra *five* days of vacation would be granted—a strong incentive for employees to take advantage of the offer. In addition, accompanied by the emphatic statement that "Vacation is an obligation not a benefit," a strict policy of NO work emails during vacation time (unless a true emergency arises) was introduced.

The results were resoundingly positive. First of all, only one person did not take the fourteen-day stretch and that was only in order to carry it to the next year to be able to take a special three week stretch. Barnekow witnessed all employees coming back from their two-week "real" vacation refreshed and reenergized, as well as enthusiastic to be back and raring to go!

In parallel, other personalized employee benefits were developed, further detailed, or updated, which were aligned with the values and approach that are communicated in their "company manifesto" and echoed in the vacation policy. These include key elements such as workplace flexibility—already an essential part of the company's work style—parental leave, and monthly performance reviews.

Sample perks floated in the survey, which resonated and were granted are:

- Gym membership: Emphasizing employees' health, a capped subsidy is offered to the gym of the individual's choice.

- Volunteering day: Building on the company's community spirit, every employee may take one workday to volunteer in their community, hopefully along with colleagues.

- Employee education: Showing that developing their potential matters, each employee is sent to one business-related course a year. Importantly, the employee has control of the course choice—the area, skills, or whatever they want to develop, career-wise.

- Passion projects: Engaging employees by encouraging them to dive into an area of the business they have a specific interest in, even outside their scope of work, and then having them share their new knowledge with everyone else.

It is key to note that some of these have low or no costs but bring great benefit to the company by supporting and augmenting the health, participation, sense of purpose, or potential of each of the employees. There are many other elements that were included in the survey but were not found to be as important to the team members of this particular company. Overall, the combination of these specific benefits was created to serve and support the well-being of all employees, thereby allowing them to perform their best for the company. The company continues its dynamic expansion as a result.

Every organization employs a unique group of people, and therefore there is a different combination of benefits that is going to move the needle for each specific workforce group. Companies have begun to focus on the impact of employees' financial situations and their "financial wellness." For most people, money can be a huge source of anxiety and distraction. If workers are preoccupied and stressed, they are not going to be giving their job the same amount of attention or consideration. Sharing information about financial management has been shown to improve employee satisfaction and engagement—with both increased attention at work and loyalty to the company providing this benefit. Whether holding a "lunch and learn" for workers to learn more about financial planning or any other business topic, training in both work- and life-related subjects has been revealed to be helpful in enhancing employee performance. In fact, 27 percent of companies plan to provide financial-related wellness support over the next three years for their employees.[72]

With so much changing so fast at work, investing in your people so that they can continually enhance and update their business knowledge—about technology, software, or new developments in different areas—is critical in the pursuit of company-wide progress. Static, status quo knowledge will quickly be out of date and, therefore, detrimental to the future of your business. There are new online learning and development offerings on a wide variety of topics in different media forms—text, graphics, audio, and video—to address the varying needs of your business and preferences of employees. Providing these solutions, which may be consumed whenever desired, can help employees keep up with changes and continue to make meaningful contributions to the company's growth.

360 DEGREES OF WELL-BEING

There are many aspects to employees' well-being, encircling their mental, physical and situational health, which are all important to consider in your overall strategic talent-focused plan. To address mental and physical elements, there are numerous options that your company may provide, encourage, and support to suit your particular worker population, such as meditation, yoga, volunteering, financial planning, nutrition, and, for all, fully-utilized vacations and "proper" sleep.

To improve employee health and engagement, sleep is a vital component as well. "Sleep is a time of intense neurological activity—a rich time of renewal, memory consolidation, brain and neurochemical cleansing, and cognitive maintenance." From Arianna Huffington's book *The Sleep Revolution*. Huffington has long been a leading voice advocating for sleep as a critical contributor to workers' well-being. She introduced two nap rooms at the Huffington Post offices in 2011 and believes we are in the midst of a "sleep deprivation crisis" and need to rethink attitudes to sleep, work, and life. Indeed, this is part Huffington's Future-of-Work-related vision and mission—embodied in her new company, Thrive Global—to reframe and broaden what success means for us all as professionals and human beings and how we achieve it.

There is a long list of attractive add-ons that companies can utilize, but the most effective perks depend on the individual. Workers do not need to take advantage of everything in order to be happy or more productive, but personalized benefits are increasingly common in the battle to improve work culture and engage employees. It certainly behooves your company to understand the types of benefits employees want and the types of accommodations or help they may need. That way, you can ensure your efforts are focused appropriately to incentivize employees' performance efforts and improve their overall happiness and productivity in the workplace. In the end, employees stay with the companies they trust and feel respected by, that are loyal to them, upfront with them, and are willing to invest in their career development and personal well-being. Period.[73]

Progress to Personalization

To accelerate setting up a personalized work environment, proactive involvement of managers and their teams is essential. Facilitated workshops and coaching can bring focus, recommendations, and clarity to the discussions and development of personalized and team-oriented plans. Here are some of the questions that will help your managers gain insights into employees' work and life in general. The answers can then be incorporated with other shared understandings from the employee and team members to create a personalized working profile:

- What kind of work do they enjoy the most, and what do they think they are best at?

- When do they find they are most productive, most focused, most "in the zone"? What times of day are best, and is one particular location better than any other?

- What are the typical weekly and daily hours and the location of an employee's current work, including if and when they work off-site?

- Do they have a desire or need to work remotely for some or more hours a week or simply shift their office hours? If so, how many hours and which day(s)? If desired, have they tried working remotely before?

- Whom do they usually work closely with? How, when, and where are these team members working, and how often do they need to collaborate in any given week?

- What non-company elements may impact their relationship with work, such as commuting, physical disabilities, or child or elder care needs, and what personal responsibilities or activities do they wish to disclose that might influence their working profile?

The very purpose of a personalized working profile is to reveal what people actually want or need from their work situation in order to be happy and motivated to be productive. This is why it is so useful for effective engagement and management. It will be up to the leadership, however, to provide the tools and environment in which employees can thrive as work and projects evolve.

As a group that is less tethered to legacy habits, perceptions, and norms of how things were done in the past, younger recruits often adjust more smoothly to new ways of working than older generations. However, they will likely still need assistance in gathering the information they need to define their optimal working profile. Meantime, Baby Boomers are proactively looking for new working solutions as they transition out of full-time work or seek ways to keep one foot in the business world as longer lives stretch funds and push retirement years further out.

There is no denying that strategizing about, developing, and implementing updated and customized work environments for each employee is a multidimensional and complex project that requires thought, time, and investment. Luckily, there are countless studies to validate the positive results that will be the reward—to your company and employees alike—if executed thoughtfully, with support for employees. The *Workplace Flexibility Toolkit* found on the U.S. Department of Labor's website can reaffirm this with supporting data.

In fact, since June 2014, the "Right to Request Flexible Working" has been *mandatory* in the U.K. for all employees who have been employed by the same employer for more than twenty-six weeks.[74] It was rolled out successfully across segments of the workforce starting in 2002, with each new segment achieving positive results.

However, if approached superficially, the numerous benefits that can accrue across the board will not materialize, and a frustrated and shrinking workforce is a likely result. Every company is different, with its own group of people, creating a particular combination of circumstances that need to be addressed with a solution that is unique to that organization.

As explained earlier, as we are in the midst of transition, inherently backward-looking "best practices" are best yielded to decisions made based on "first principles." For many of the personalization elements—eg, workplace flexibility and new benefits—the way to achieve a smooth and successful transition is to take an incremental approach to implementation. Trials can roll out new aspects in different divisions, each time evaluating and adjusting based on the specific scenarios playing out among those particular team members and allowing different adoption rates to alleviate individuals' anxieties of reworking familiar structures.

Having carefully identified how your company can best assess productivity and ways to personalize employees' work and formats, individual performances will tell you how successful your efforts have been. The trial periods can be used, carefully, to monitor whether various modifications are helping any particular employee to be more productive once they have settled into a new work pattern.

It is worth remembering that some employees may perform less well while they adjust or if they have inadvertently chosen a new work situation that does not actually support their preferred working style. For example, some people find working from home feels too isolated, or they get too easily distracted. So, certain adjustments will occur to find the right combination, not just for each person but for combinations of employees who are interdependent and need to coordinate their desired scenarios so they can work effectively with whomever and from wherever and are supported.

All told, with the current evolving workplace dynamics, there is new emphasis, even an imperative focus, on engaging the workforce to improve productivity and performance in order for your company to stay competitive in the marketplace. This may involve reassessing current talent management, operating practices, and business models, combined with a willingness to undertake some fundamental changes. Focused on talent performance, Barnekow's modifications to vacation policies were first intended to give his employees the critical foundation of good health. This, in turn, bolstered employees' overall energy and efforts to support the ambitious growth plans he was keen to achieve.

Creating personalized and adaptable work frameworks and functions permit the maximizing of individuals'—and by extension also the company's—potential. It is no longer a matter of *smarter* business strategy; it is likely to be the *only* viable strategy companies will have to survive the quantity of changes taking place around them.

Chapter 6 Takeaways

- **First Principles**: Step back and examine what basic elements are important for understanding and generating productivity and success at your company—at unit (team, department, or division) levels and for the business overall. Explore what data would be relevant to measure these elements—with a combination of qualitative and quantitative metrics, considering knowledge worker productivity especially. Contemplate how data could be gathered most effectively to be used in a timely manner. Evaluate how performance could best be enhanced, as well as gauged in a manner that is useful on an ongoing basis, especially in a fast-moving and evolving marketplace.

- **Priorities:**

  □ Engagement—Enhanced engagement results in increased productivity and performance. Assessing how to measure the components of individuals' engagement is essential in order to support, track, and refine initiatives for boosting workers' performance and productivity.

  □ Personalization—Performance reviews are increasing in frequency, creating more relevant and timely feedback loops to absorb learnings in a more timely manner to improve performance going forward. These proactive ongoing individual discussions also enhance employer/employee relationships through increased support and collaboration.

  □ Integration—Productivity is enhanced when departments are closely-coordinated, working together to support employees. All employees—office-based and remote workers—are best integrated thoughtfully into the performance system for monitoring as well as for recognition and promotion purposes.

▫ Choice—Measurement data is plentiful; however, careful choice of metrics is critical for an actual understanding of your business and the relative and overall performance of the talent that drives its growth.

- **Evaluation:**

  ▫ How many qualitative elements are included in your metrics to assess engagement, productivity, and performance?

  ▫ Have you assessed the effectiveness of using ratings at your company for performance reviews, if ratings are currently used?

  ▫ How often are you doing performance reviews?

  ▫ Is your remote workers' performance monitored differently from your office-based employees?

  ▫ How well are project details and deliverables communicated to employees working remotely?

  ▫ Has your company considered or developed a means to track group/team performance?

  ▫ How many of your workers have done tests to identify their strengths or personality traits? Have these been used by managers to modify employees' work content?

  ▫ Have you yet surveyed your employees to understand what benefits would resonate with them?

  ▫ Do the company executives take all their vacation?

  ▫ What percentage of employees takes all their vacation days?

□ What learning and development options are offered to your employees—how up-to-date are they and how are they delivered and consumed?

□ What percentage of your workers take advantage of them?

- **Metrics**: Examples include: Number of performance reviews done per employee in a year; rate of promotion of remote-working employees relative to office-based workers; number of events per year creating a sense of community across all employees; percentage of employees and independent contractors who have completed personality tests and ascertained their specific strengths; increase in percentage of employees who have been coached to evaluate their optimal working profile and style; percentage of employees participating in a survey about employee preferences and benefits; increase in percentage of employees taking all their vacation days; increase in learning and development choices offered to employees; and increase in percentage of employees availing themselves of these options.

CHAPTER 7

MINDSET, POLICIES, AND ENVIRONMENT

Progress is impossible without change, and those who cannot change their minds cannot change anything.

GEORGE BERNARD SHAW

The 86 Company has an inspirational company manifesto, which establishes the vision, purpose, and values of the company, directing and guiding the behaviors and actions of the passionate employees who work there. It includes elements that help describe the mindset of team members, explaining *how* they are approaching and accomplishing their goals: "We inspire, teach, and share … We are courageous and do things in an unexpected fashion."

Focused on rapid growth, CEO Malte Barnekow needed to attract the right people as well as keep his existing team intact, while fostering creativity and high-quality work. He wanted everyone at the company to have, or certainly be comfortable with, the bold attitude that their pioneering goals generally required if they were to be achieved. However, laggard company policies—such as no paid parental leave—would be incongruent with such a groundbreaking approach, potentially distracting and even undermining employees' focus and alignment with the business objectives. Consequently, their employee handbook and benefits were expanded and updated to ensure they communicated a consistent message internally, and externally for attracting suitable recruits.

We are living in an increasingly fast-moving world. Change is becoming a constant, and disruption is almost the norm. The makeup of the S&P 500 is changing faster than ever, with the average lifetime of Fortune 500 companies on it dropping from seventy-five years to fifteen over the last half-century and still declining.[75] We are moving away from the closed, rigid, and compartmentalized structures and processes of the early Industrial Age, toward corporate ecosystems that are open and flexible, transformed by technology to be interconnected and interdependent.

At the core of your ecosystem is your company's mindset, which in turn is translated into the corporate policies that reflect and support it. It is important that these policies are well-harmonized, as well as recognizing the influence of the evolving externalities on the ecosystem. As an example, the 86 Company's manifesto captures the company's mindset and articulates its culture and values and the guiding principles of its bold and creative mission. The company's policies are then coherent with their attitude, reinforcing their values, which are communicated consistently externally as well as being responsive to significant prevailing external factors.

All About Attitude

Mindset matters. It is important to understand that the corporate "attitude" or mindset is the thinking culture of your organization. It is the mental expression of the values your company is built on. It dictates and influences the behaviors that are active manifestations of your company's culture, embodied in the policies it composes. When expressed consistently and purposefully, employees can easily interpret the culture, and the mindset component, of the organization and feel comfortable in their work environment.

We are probably all in the process of absorbing the effect of our increasingly blended professional and personal circumstances—how they are fundamentally changing, and how we might decide to approach the new scenarios we are facing. Whatever attitude we each choose as "appropriate" becomes paramount when leading our team(s) or company through these transitional times, so that new ideas can be considered thoughtfully, with the real possibility of adapting or replacing the old ones.

Early industrial-era production processes were linear, and linear thinking was commonplace too. As noted in chapter 1, starting in the 1800s, the schooling of our workforce ingrained a conforming mindset with limited divergence, in deliberate preparation for the easy management of factory workers. Radical "out-of-the-box" creativity was not welcomed, except in the specifically-designated "innovation departments" or research labs. The deliberate consequence was the raising of generations of workers capable of accepting—but likely not being engaged in—meaningless or repetitious work. The paycheck was the reward. Period.

Circumstances have evolved. First of all, the supporting "machine layer" is now sensory, not just mechanical, with touch screens that are more intuitive. It is also far more powerful, networked, and mobile. The exponential increase of computing power, as we recognize in Moore's law, has led to the acceleration of the pace of business—but fixed corporate organizational structures and mindsets do not have the flexibility or capacity to deal with the implications of the very frequency of information updates.

"How would you like to be the VP of Medieval Thinking?"

The sheer volume of data now is increasing exponentially, no matter what data your company is currently tracking and analyzing. An adaptable and open approach is best-suited for scrutinizing this information usefully, with a perspective that is as neutral—and therefore as objective—as possible, in order to understand the full range of possibilities and interpret them effectively. If constrained by less-flexible mindsets, executives and their workers likely struggle to assimilate the fundamental changes related to digitally-activated interconnectedness and the speed with which updates and iterations are occurring. This is the *Connected Economy*—"a new business reality in which value is created through technology-enabled links among people, machines, and organizations," as explained by Paulo Carvao, a general manager at IBM.[76]

This connectivity is both leveraged and optimized when internal operations are sufficiently responsive and adaptable, through expanding integration and rising communication between divisions. So employees are increasingly working in cross-functional teams to develop and deliver client solutions—breaking down internal and departmental silos. The 86 Company has a nationally-distributed workforce that operates in a networked manner, using platform applications to share information efficiently, such as for monitoring their sales progress, tracking projects, and communicating market updates.

At the same time, employees are now encouraged to bring their whole selves to work, so that they may feel more comfortable, less constrained. This means more complex circumstances for leaders at every level of the organization to absorb and manage effectively. A talent strategy of inclusion actively embraces the type of mindset—and brings the diversity of thought—that is best able to handle the richer and dynamic environment successfully. As part of the culture, shared values may allow a range of perspectives that attract and accommodate the broad variety of aligned, but not like-minded, individuals who are suitable for *your* company.

The mindset of each hire also has an impact. Each of us arrives at any office with our own personal context, combining our history, background, experiences, and opinions. My own is many-flavored—originally British, now an American citizen, I have lived and worked around the world—including the U.K., Hong Kong, Germany, and now the United States. I am a Generation-X female, a mother, an MBA graduate, and a business owner. With the appropriate mindset,

I can be very thoughtful about how, where, and to what extent these aspects influence my viewpoint and decision-making. I also make great efforts to acknowledge and respect the context of anyone I interact with—whatever their age, race, generation, and background, and whatever perspectives they bring to the table.

Some of the younger members of the workforce are bringing visibility to certain mindsets and approaches that are influencing a more thorough rethinking of work routines and the concept of work itself, as mentioned in chapter 3. Any reevaluation of the essence and meaning of work—the "why," as well as the "what" and "how"— influences the corporate mindset. This is resulting in a composition of the corporate culture that elevates certain elements of purpose and passion in the for-profit landscape that have historically been mostly absent. Policies that accommodate these new cultural dimensions may be more effective with certain employees and groups. Managing through, and with, meaning can give supervisors new ways to motivate and engage your workforce and attract new talent.

Translating Mindset to Policy

At the core of the ecosystem, culture, mindset, and values collectively create, inform, and influence the context for every individual, as well as the corporation as a whole. The essence of these perspectives is important, then, to be reflected in the formal framework—i.e., the internal corporate policies—as the 86 Company realized.

A mindset that is inclusive and adaptable for the cultural environment and marketplace is then appropriately extended to be inclusive and adaptable to the worker as an individual. When policies can accommodate personal preferences, style, needs, and openness, it is a gesture of recognition and concern for the worker that boosts not only individual performance but also workplace morale. For example, a workplace flexibility policy is focused on understanding and accommodating employees' work preferences and styles in order to better engage them. The flexibility that a company can show to its employees helps in conveying respect and trust for the individual, including stimulating a greater sense of responsibility and accountability for their work.

Thus, workplace flexibility is a matter of mindset first and policy second. Whatever the policy that executives, managers, or documents may state, without the accompanying open and adaptable mindset, workplace flexibility will likely be executed superficially. When it is implemented effectively, members of management are genuinely on board, and their mindset is communicated through detailed, thorough, and supported execution with consistent follow-up. Only an authentic intent to address each employee's needs and flexibility will be properly integrated as a strategic new mode of operating.

Otherwise, the rewards—of your employees feeling respected, valued, and trusted, and your company reaping the reciprocal benefits of the workforce's increased engagement, productivity, and loyalty—will not be achieved. There are innumerable studies that support the validity of the benefits that accrue. One of the early large studies—of over seven hundred firms in the U.S., the U.K., France, and Germany—found a significant positive relationship between work-life-balance practices and total-factor productivity.[77]

That is not to say that workplace-flexibility policies are easy to implement—they are the manifestation of a fundamental shift to engage employees on an individual basis. Workplace flexibility therefore often means moving from fixed working structures to frameworks and processes that allow managers and workers to coordinate personalized schedules and the tasks they are working on, individually and in teams. Fortunately, the numerous studies and countless beneficial results experienced by U.K. companies have repeatedly demonstrated the powerful positive impact of workplace flexibility.

As mentioned in chapter 6, the "Right to Request Flexible Working" has been mandatory in U.K. companies since June 2014. It was initially rolled out with a small segment of the population in 2003. At that time, only working parents with children under six years old were given the right to request some flexibility in their weekly work schedule. The request process starts with the onus on the employees to propose the type of flexibility they desire— that may not have a detrimental impact on the business—and the company has nine official reasons for refusing the request. However, more than three-quarters of requests were typically granted, and the beneficial results experienced by employers led to successive expansions of the law. Over slightly more than a decade, it was rolled out to include additional employee segments, until finally it became enacted nationwide. The application and review process between employer and employee is very well thought through and worth reading if you are interested in implementing workplace flexibility in a meaningful way in your company.[78]

Even as a policy is an official form of the mindset company-wide, it can still be implemented in a customizable way, which becomes a theme where the objective is progress. Top-down, "blanket" workplace-flexibility policies do not fit everyone. Policies may be applied without the intent to personalize, that are actually driven by a singular emphasis of benefit to the company—such as cost cutting or ease of implementation. In these cases, where there is little or no consideration for the personal situations of the employees, few benefits are achieved, and problems may result instead.

However, adaptations can be made to focus on the audiences that are receptive to that specific benefit. In 2013, as part of a corporate directive to save on real estate costs, American Express changed a major group of call-center and travel-related jobs to telecommuting only. This would obviously be challenging for anyone living in a tiny apartment with small children. So, the hiring strategy going forward became focused on those who actively wanted, and could support, an entirely home-based job. The company's Axcess@Home now targets telecommuters specifically and is tailored to support a large remote workforce.

Aetna is another example of a company with policy-making that was introduced and aligned with the corporate mindset. After having a terrible ski accident in 2004, CEO Mark Bertolini spent roughly a year out of the office as he fought to recover. He tried everything to aid and accelerate his recuperation—homeopathic techniques, yoga, and meditation—and he made a much faster and fuller recovery than doctors had anticipated. When he returned to work, he brought a new mindset and inclusive approach to health and wellness to the company and started yoga and meditation for everybody who wanted to participate. By the time 28 percent of people had taken any of the classes, there had been a sufficient reduction in stress and increase in the wellness of workers that Aetna decreased their health-care costs by nearly $7 million; this was in addition to the benefits of heightened focus and productivity that new studies show can be attributed to meditation.

Policies that are thorough in trying to execute effectively upon something that is consistent with the mindset are most likely to achieve the desired benefits if some flexibility is included within the policy's framework, allowing for people to adapt. In addition, successful adoption occurs when corporate executives support the policies emphatically and set the examples to follow.

The objective is not to change everything, but rather, using first principles, to identify what really makes sense to modify for your company and employees in order to create the circumstances that will yield the best overall results. It does take work to discover which elements to keep and which new ones to adopt, and then to test and tweak until your company achieves the fertile work environment it is striving for.

A first step is recognizing the mindset that will embrace progress and start to improve the work environment. Managers and leaders who succeed in recognizing, respecting, and supporting employees at an individual level can build fuller, more interactive relationships that yield greater reciprocity, and policies can be amended to reflect and support this approach, just as American Express and Aetna did.

Evolving the Ecosystem

As modifications are made to improve the internal corporate circumstances, it is imperative also to recognize other external factors that are in the process of transforming the broader corporate environment from a policy perspective.

As mentioned in chapter 1, many of the current U.S. labor and employment laws were written and enacted at least half a century ago, and society has evolved significantly since then, such that now the need to update the laws has become increasingly urgent. The United States is also now lagging behind many countries in important areas of workers' rights—including paid sick leave and paid vacation time—and is the only industrialized nation still without mandatory paid parental leave.[79] In contrast to Europe, where the government remains the determinant of critical labor policies, in the United States the private sector is left to take care of many workers' rights and needs. U.S. labor unions, which used to drive key policy terms, have lost much of their power and influence over the past several decades.

However, following the U.K.'s example and findings relating to workplace flexibility, in June 2014 President Obama signed a presidential memorandum introducing the flexible working options for government employees.[80] The same month, Scott Stringer, comptroller of New York, put a proposal forward advocating for private-sector workplace flexibility, with the specific purpose of being able to continue to attract the top talent to the state of New York.

Then, just as the government appeared compelled to make or recommend sweeping changes, some major policy changes were announced in the private sector. In August 2015, three major corporations—Adobe, Microsoft, and Netflix—changed their parental-leave policies. Adobe started to offer between sixteen and twenty-six weeks. Microsoft offered up to twenty weeks, eight more than they did before. Netflix was particularly remarkable in giving a year to the parent, who has great flexibility to work part-time or full-time on different occasions over the course of the year.

What is important to note is that these companies understood, just as the 86 Company did, that to create a compelling working environment that would engage and retain the talent they needed, incongruent policies were not sustainable long term. Working to establish attractive cultures, it was appropriate to update important policies to be in alignment.

For your company—just as with other aspects of the total compensation package—consider how your key policies will be thought of when compared with your competitors. Your company may increasingly be judged relative to these additional criteria—by your existing employees or others you wish to attract to work at your company. It is preferable—and less expensive—to update policies *before* attrition has risen or hiring is challenged. As a general principle, remain aware of all the changes taking place in the business ecosystem. Some of these will impact you as an employer more than others, but effective policies depend on good information and foresight to guide them.

Progress means recognizing the evolving ecosystem and enriching the overall work environment, which is a multifaceted process. It involves the many elements of culture, mindset, personalization, benefits, and more, all integrated to create a healthy habitat for all your employees, and by means of which your company may grow stronger. Mindsets are shifting with the Future-of-Work developments. So, policies may be revised in order to reflect these changes, thought through and carefully implemented to realize their benefits and ensure that they are viable for the long term and can adapt as transformation progresses. Your culture and ecosystem will thrive when you do.

Chapter 7 Takeaways

- **First Principles**: Consider what mindset will allow your company to be sufficiently flexible and adaptable in the fast-paced marketplace. Review how well the culture and mindset of your company are connected and communicated, as well as reflected in the behaviors of your workforce. Develop (or modify) consistent policies as extensions of the culture and mindset. Monitor the external environment for changes that could impact your business model or operating practices, including policies.

- **Priorities**:

  - Engagement—Employees' attitudes, as well as those of prospective hires, are best aligned with the company culture. This promotes a cohesive culture as well as connection with the organization and within the community and steers policy-making that is aligned for the benefit of your workforce.

  - Personalization—The company's mindset resonates with each employee differently, while aligning them strategically and guiding them operationally. These differences are embraced, while context setting helps comprehension and incorporation of all perspectives.

  - Integration—The Connected Economy is driving the breaking down of barriers between departments to facilitate seamless collaboration and cross-functional teams. Monitoring the external ecosystem for possible changes ahead in the employment and labor laws is advisable, as is watching the general business environment.

  - Choice—With a strong culture and clearly-understood mindset, employees can most easily make choices that are directed at a high level by the range of understood parameters.

- **Evaluation**:

  - How clearly is the mindset of your company understood internally?

  - How much are prospective hires tested for alignment with the corporate culture and mindset?

  - How well is the mindset reflected in all your corporate policies? Is there any incongruence?

▫ What workplace flexibility options are offered at your company?

▫ How well are the workplace flexibility choices proactively shared and explained to employees?

▫ Do all employees use these options?

▫ How well are employees working remotely supported in their work and promoted in the organization?

▫ How many of your company's policies allow customization or personalization?

- **Metrics**: Examples include: Increase in (relevant) percentage of teams with cross-functional members; percentage decrease in average expression of work-life conflict at your company; increase in employee use of workplace flexibility options; increase in percentage of personalization options associated with key talent-related corporate policies; and increase in percentage of employees using customized options of company policies.

CHAPTER 8

CREATIVITY AND COLLABORATION

I know I've made some very poor decisions recently, but I can give you my complete assurance that my work will be back to normal. I've still got the greatest enthusiasm and confidence in the mission. And I want to help you.

HAL 9000, FROM *2001: A SPACE ODYSSEY*

We are moving into an age of increasingly-advanced artificial intelligence, robotics, and automation. However, despite the delightful robot dogs and cat-scaring robot vacuum cleaners, we still have not yet attained the sophisticated quasi-human equivalent of "general artificial intelligence" that HAL was capable of in Stanley Kubrick's 1968 movie *2001: A Space Odyssey*. Although, apparently, we are close now.

Kai Goerlich, Chief Futurist at SAP's Innovation Center Network, described the essence of "human genius" to me[81] using the analogy of a jazz band, where the musicians gather around a creative moment and respond to the imaginative, and spontaneous, energy of each artist's melody. This is in contrast to an orchestra that's governed by the sheet music that each musician must follow—which in many ways is similar to the defined, sequential, linear dimensions of the programming of most of today's industrial robots. However, the fuzzy logic of the most advanced independently acting robots is (or will be soon) testing these distinctions.

We are faced with a challengingly competitive world—for market share of products, services, and talent. The companies that will excel going forward will be the ones that have managed to engage and stimulate all members of their workforce as "humans" in the most productive way. Considering Maslow's hierarchy of needs,[82] your "human" workers will be most effective in their creative efforts when you are able to provide a holistic environment in which their needs are fulfilled and they are fully supported. This means mentally, physically, emotionally, and functionally, during their periods of individual concentration as well as group collaboration.

Embracing Range and Risks

Stimulating human creativity may sound simpler than it is. First of all, it depends on having an understanding of what humans are best at specifically, and many corporations have expended little effort in developing that across their workforce. Human beings are good at spontaneous ideation and nonlinear thought as opposed to repetitive action, excelling at nonsequential, "out-of-the-box" thinking in ways that, at least for now, very few robots are. Humans have "inspiration" and "gut" feelings about ideas and directions that can lead to non-incremental, unforeseeable change.[83]

"We call out to you, please reveal yourself oh
Spirit of Innovation"

Personalized attention and adaptation are fundamental parameters in providing the appropriate setup and surroundings for your workers to thrive in. As noted earlier, corporate culture is at the core, so an essential element is proactively promoting a culture that celebrates and enables creativity and the different modes and manners in which this may be catalyzed. Cultural tenets include diversity and inclusion, an embracing of exploration and experimentation, a willingness to take risks, and an accommodation of failure.

An inclusive approach—encompassing diversity of gender, race, age, and other dimensions[84]—is paramount to enable the fullest breadth of possibilities to be explored in a meaningful way. Creativity is boosted if employees are encouraged to express diversity of thought and perspectives and allowed to act on independent thinking.

The Science of Inclusion[85] provides evidence that diverse and inclusive teams are more creative and make better decisions. It also confirms that humans have a biologically-based need to belong— to feel included, supported, and valued by others socially. So, an inclusive culture extends to how employees and other workers involved in the creative process are treated and how the environment supports social cohesion. In fact, research shows that social exclusion can negatively impact performance and productivity. This has stimulated new efforts to ensure that innovation teams include a range of perspectives in order to optimize opportunities to generate the best ideas possible.

It is essential to have leaders who are willing to encourage employees to take an idea and thoughtfully develop and test it, with the possibility that it might fail. The key then is to learn from unsuccessful projects, incorporate the new understanding, adapt, and improve. At the same time, leadership can ensure there is clear comprehension and communication about what is intelligent and reasonable risk, for which appropriate criteria can be established—such as the amount spent on a project with a certain risk profile under specific conditions.

New attitudes to risk and independent thinking are being adopted in corporate settings, too, to encourage creativity. There has been popular promotion of entrepreneurial approaches, or so-called "intrapreneurial" thinking, relating to project work to try to reap the benefits of more diverse thinking and greater risk taking. Sometimes innovation teams are located offsite, away from the main corporate offices, to help distance themselves mentally from the typical corporate mindset.

Stimulating and Supportive Environments

Corporate culture is articulated in words, expressed in actions, and reflected in the environment itself. These days an open and inclusive culture would be hard to reconcile with a workplace that is mostly comprised of private offices. Employees are intuitively comfortable with surroundings that are harmonious with the culture, or similarly they may be consciously or subconsciously disoriented by discrepancies between the culture and the environment. Such inconsistencies do not support creativity. The workplace itself is the physical manifestation of a company's culture, and so diversity and inclusion are also best expressed physically by the type and variety of layouts and arrangements that are offered. Google and Facebook are well known for embracing a strategy that expresses their culture through their work environment.

Foosball tables have been ridiculed in their seeming symbolic representation of younger workers not being serious about their work. However, they are visible expressions of corporate cultures that willingly acknowledge and welcome the full spectrum of their employees' work and leisure activities and needs. In addition, the reality is that such furnishings encourage people to take a break and enjoy themselves and then return to work. What is more, some of the best creative moments are anecdotally reported to have occurred during periods of office-based leisure activity, when people's minds are differently occupied.

An essential piece of the puzzle is recognition of the dynamics of work. Architects and workplace designers were perhaps the first groups of professionals to observe the reality of workers' daily needs. For decades, office layouts were configured with only cubicles and conference rooms. However, studies then revealed that the workstations had low utilization rates. In 2003, Cisco reported that 65 percent of their workstations were vacant.[86] At Sun Microsystems, 35 percent of employees were not working in their assigned building, never mind workspace, and at ABN Amro just 55 percent of workstations were observed to be occupied in 2006.[87]

Employees have not been able to accomplish all their necessary tasks effectively sitting alone in their cubicles. Research has revealed that all employees have a common set of work-related activities,[88] of which some are individual and many are collaborative—whether in pairs, larger group sessions, or ongoing project teams. Activity-Based Working (ABW) office design was established in the 1990s in response to this—the term being coined by Erik Veldhoen in his book *The Demise of the Office*. The objective was to recognize and support these activities in a more varied approach to the design and creation of the office environment, helping workers be more productive in combinations that were appropriate for that specific company and workforce.

Therefore, a company leveraging elements of Future-of-Work progress to stimulate creativity can develop a flexible and varied environment that recognizes, and also measures and promotes, the value of both individual and group work activities.[89] Proactive and adaptable support allows workers to maximize the creative potential of all relevant scenarios.

Herman Miller, a provider of furnishings and related technologies and services, is a pioneer in this field and has developed its "Living Office" system in response for the office environment. Its modular furnishings provide settings for ten identified types of work activities to promote the creative process and accomplishment of work generally. The system is designed to be flexibly configured and to accommodate the specific people working and the types of work they are doing,[90] while also recognizing and supporting their basic human needs so that they are best able to accomplish their tasks.

The optimal setup supports a comprehensive approach that encompasses a diversity of thought, talent, and venue; leverages workers' personal strengths; and considers how to adapt to, adopt, and match up different working profiles, styles, and tasks. In so doing, individuals and groups may work and collaborate where, when, and at what they do best, with the ability to modify different elements as projects evolve.[91]

Creativity does not happen in a vacuum or in a box. Practically, physical office spaces can incorporate variety by providing areas where groups can gather temporarily, where they can collaborate on tasks in long-term hubs, and where they can intersect and interact with one another by chance. These areas are in addition to places for individuals to do concentrated work in isolation or proximate to their teams, as well as the standard conference rooms that are expected in workplace layouts. Open workspaces with widely visible whiteboards are a natural way to share information about ongoing projects more broadly. These displays allow for spontaneous contributions from different people and viewpoints and encourage internal transparency, thus promoting and building trust.

Creativity in the workplace is also not about static collaboration. Modular and mobile furnishings are groundbreaking in their ability to enable a diverse and changing range of office settings, as needed. They can adjust easily for new tasks and business needs and accommodate the different approaches and working styles of the individuals or groups working on a specific current project, allowing for a fluid transfer of knowledge and ideas among and between teams.[92]

CO-WORKING

My company, Flexcel Network, has been situated in a co-working space since early 2013. Why? First of all, co-working is philosophically and practically one of the founding new Future-of-Work environments with its flexible and community nature. Second, it was important for me to experience the work setting firsthand and understand its economics, benefits, challenges, and quirks. Third, I discovered (for my own optimal working profile) that I was personally best supported by the creative energy, conversation, and camaraderie of the community of people at NeueHouse, where I work.

There are now many co-working spaces and companies which offer a range of models, cultures, targeted communities, services offered, and more. NeueHouse is just one model—a curated membership of established creative entrepreneurs and a carefully nurtured culture that works for me, where I find creativity, positive energy, and an international orientation. Large traditional companies often send internal groups there for innovation-focused off-sites, which the culture stimulates well. Some have even trialed teams working there longer-term, helping them generate new ideas when physically distant from a more staid corporate environment. Co-working spaces may now house the non-HQ/branch offices of companies of all sizes, taking advantage of more flexible office-leasing arrangements. I expect many more of these types of scenarios going forward.

Could a co-working location be beneficial for some of your workers or to replace one of your smaller offices and/or be used to provide an off-site creative environment for one or more of your teams? Explore the alternatives—each one has a different economic model, environment, ambiance, and community type. Pick one that suits your company's culture, workers, and business model.

As a project develops, a team working together may need to bring in other colleagues from different departments or outside consultants to contribute. So, a team's "home" space may need to expand and contract, depending on who is working, from where and when, what they are doing, and how the project is evolving. Embracing the mobility of work will enhance the prospects for inspiration. With less rigidity in the physical workplace, the workflow can also be more spontaneous and flexible. A flexible approach from leadership can maximize employee collaboration and production. Sakara and Big Ass Solutions are great examples of companies with many cross-functional teams collaborating to leverage relevant skills as needed for more complex or extensive projects.

In parallel, the marketplace is continually evolving—customers are more informed and demanding, dynamic feedback loops lead to frequent incremental product iterations and service enhancements—and projects are following the changing circumstances. There is increasing demand for internal and external agility to stay ahead of disruptive start-ups and competition. Companies embracing progress are better able to recognize the ongoing state of change and the unprecedented operational flexibility that is able to accommodate it and thrive within it. This new level of responsiveness is achievable with integrated and coordinated internal operations that leverage a cohesive and coherent cultural, physical, and technically-current environment.

Supplying the Tools

Technology is an essential supporter of today's creativity and collaboration in both physical and virtual environments, as noted in chapter 2, with workers becoming increasingly mobile and dispersed—temporarily or long term. In the office, practical elements of technology, such as adequate overhead, underfoot, or movable electrical outlets and smart boards, are the most basic components of the mobile- and modular-enabled creative environment. In addition, more sophisticated characteristics of physical space that promote inventive thought and interaction are best extended and echoed in the virtual corporate space. It is important to replicate in the business environment the seamless interconnectedness and versatile ingenuity of applications that employees are experiencing as consumers, facilitating virtual work.

Appropriate new applications, devices, and platforms can be identified by internal or external IT specialists, who can enable the types of interaction and collaboration relevant for your company. It is especially valuable to be able to connect, communicate, and interact with workers not based in the office, temporarily or permanently. Platforms and applications can be selected to allow workers to collaborate and complete tasks virtually, mimicking aspects of in-person collaboration and interaction; examples of this include Skype, Google+, GoToMeeting, WebEx, Slack, Trello, and Asana.

These types of tools also create peer-to-peer connections that can span functions and business units as well as physical space. The communication thus enabled promotes enhanced integration among teams and their members, wherever they are and whatever department or division they might belong to. In addition, people have different sets of skills and work in different ways, and technology is allowing more options for how to address, cater to, or compromise about those differences.

A variety of applications might also be used depending on the project, the type of work involved, or the people participating on the team—from video and visualization tools to project-management tracking and measurement tools, appropriate for different types of tasks and projects. Different tools have different uses and can be very specific to one type of task or person, which highlights how technology can facilitate, and even optimize, work processes and achievement.

In order to provide the mobile- and integrated-technology support that will foster the creativity and collaboration desired to compete successfully, thoughtful technical integration is a priority. Collaboration is also necessary for the core digital innovation. In order for companies to execute their digital-integration strategies with any coherent effect, they need to work together extensively—interacting internally across functions and teams. Long-established silos between divisions and departments prevent IT from optimizing its new strategic role. The impact of dismantling these perceived barriers is already shown by much higher revenues at companies that have already made significant progress integrating across divisions to facilitate and promote collaboration.[93]

Such facilitation is becoming easier as technology continues to synchronize with our needs and invent new possibilities that enable a better version of our current work experience. The digitally-enhanced work environment is now more intuitive, adaptable, and highly-networked, adding new power and dimension to collaboration possibilities.

There is so much more that technological advances can and will bring to work environments to morph and disrupt, such that processes and practices—including how, when, and where creativity and collaboration are best achieved—will frequently evolve as a necessity. The interplay of "real" and "virtual" itself—and the decreasing delineation between the two—has an impact. The connectivity, independence, and immediacy of the digital workplace also alter the needs, preferences, and expectations people have in the physical one, as well as how and where they choose to interact and communicate.

Whatever the size of your company (especially when you do not have an IT department or have one that is not especially business- or process-oriented yet), it can be very beneficial to solicit the input of a handful of employees who are well-versed in business-focused applications and software. They can assist in identifying, tracking, and testing the potential of emerging applications and software to anticipate what is important and what might be ahead.

At the same time, as mentioned in chapter 2, "shadow IT" is a lurking danger for those companies that do not proactively address their IT evolution and find appropriate enterprise solutions. Many employees will find new ad hoc ways of working, using new and inventive applications rather than relying on business applications that have not been upgraded or are misaligned or not available.

In such situations, the greatest possible issue is security, considering the rise of debilitating and/or costly cyber attacks and hacks. So, preemptive attention should be paid to avoid these risks. That said, there might be select areas or occasions where workers are permitted to use personal devices or consumer applications to assist or enhance their creativity and share their discoveries or collaborate with their colleagues. I recommend that these be identified, defined, and specified.

The enhanced digital interconnectedness does not just offer alternatives to where and when people can work. Having a seamless digital network has greatly expanded the scope of whom you can do business with, and there is evidence to show the increased business success that can result.[94] In addition, it is now much easier for small businesses to collaborate and partner with each other, even across great physical divides, allowing different approaches, specialties, cultures, and perspectives to energize the creative process.

Using platforms that are company-size independent or agnostic also enables connections and collaboration between all sizes of organizations, to leverage strengths in niche markets, scale, quality elements, distribution, manufacturing, or some other type of service or product, without having to sacrifice independence in exchange. Bringing people together, no matter what their angle or lens may be, is beneficial not only to the final product but also in crafting better strategies and techniques for future projects.

Uniting all these elements succesfully—workers, environment, and tools—is the critical combination for creativity and collaboration, which can be maximized when a strong and integrated relationship between HR, FM (facilities management), and IT is prioritized. Leaders can then ensure that the optimal tools and processes are being used, relative to the ways work is accomplished and the activities of different people and teams. Moreover, the relevant physical spaces are understood, coherent, and executed appropriately between and among all departments. At the same time, we are not forgetting to maintain consistency with the company's culture and purpose. The creative collaboration you are hoping for can only be as powerful as the cohesive environment to support it, otherwise discord will manifest itself within the workplace and results will suffer.

Returning to the very essence of our human creativity, after interviewing SAP's Goerlich and understanding his perspective—comparing and contrasting humans and robots—it seems clear that this is a seminal moment in our evolution. Robots are helping us work out what it really means to be human and, by extension, truly creative.

We will thrive when we recognize, embrace, and nurture the essence of these characteristics that truly differentiate us from each other and from robots. So, it's about moving on from rigid, machine-like types of working attitudes and situations—a dramatic departure from Henry Ford's factory production lines. The emphasis is now on cultivating personalized and collaborative environments that will allow us to engage and create together and separately-in our uniquely human ways.

Chapter 8 Takeaways:

- **First Principles:** Reflect on the culture, mindset, and environment that are going to stimulate creativity at your company and enable your employees to be as "human" as possible. Consider how intelligent risk-taking might be permitted and guided appropriately. Review how failure can be responded to so that future experimentation is not discouraged or thwarted. Research how the physical environment can support creativity and collaboration, with relevant virtual extensions and connectivity. Consider developing office spaces that can optimize your workers' performance and provide integrated technology support for office-based and remote-working employees.

- **Priorities**:

  □ Engagement—A diverse and inclusive culture and physical environment will promote more creativity and better decision-making, while the opposite will undermine productivity and performance.

  □ Personalization—Encouraging your workers to bring their whole selves to work allows them to be most at ease and empowered to be creative. Office spaces that can be used for "on-demand" personalized work activities—allowing customization for the work and the person—can promote performance. Different applications and devices can support creativity and collaboration in different ways—understanding what your workers need for their particular type of work and projects can enhance their results.

- Integration—The seamless combination of workers, technology, and environment (office/home/elsewhere) can support optimal performance. Connecting and working across divisions and teams can stimulate new ideas and perspectives, boosting creativity.

- Choice—With a range of well-supported and integrated working spaces, applications, and mobile devices, workers can select the place that suits their needs to do specific creative work—for individual and group/team collaboration as needed.

- **Evaluation:**

  - How well are creativity and collaboration currently supported by your culture, the physical space in your office(s), and technically for those working remotely?

  - Does your office yet have any activity-based workspaces?

  - How well are workers equipped with mobile technology to allow them greater choice of work environment?

  - How up-to-date are the devices and applications that employees are using to accomplish their tasks?

  - How well are remote workers supported technically?

- ▫ Are your employees using consumer tools because enterprise applications are either not current or seamlessly integrated?

- ▫ How coordinated are your IT and facilities-management departments?

- ▫ Are they working with human resources to ensure relevant personalized support?

- **Metrics**: Examples include: Increase in (intelligent) risk profile of projects developed; increase in number of failed projects (within appropriate parameters); increase in successful projects born out of learning from failed experiments; increase in variety of workspaces provided; decrease in complaints by employees that technical tools, support, or appropriate meeting spaces are not sufficient or up-to-date; and increase in technical support calls provided to remote-working employees.

CHAPTER 9

FREELANCERS AND FRAMEWORKS

Freelancing lets you shift gears when the world does.
SARA HOROWITZ, FOUNDER,
FREELANCERS UNION

n 2016, nearly 38 percent of the world's workforce was considered nonemployee, up 10 percent from 2015.[95] From 2014 to 2016, the U.S. freelance workforce grew by two million workers, from fifty-three to fifty-five million. The freelance workforce earned an estimated $1 trillion from freelancing in 2015. Sixty-three percent of freelancers say they started more by choice than necessity, up from 53 percent in 2014.[96] Fifty-eight percent of companies are embracing on-demand and real-time talent sources.[97]

The composition of the labor force is shifting, as is the combination of workers who are gathering to collaborate—virtually and in person—to innovate and accomplish tasks and projects for your company. Until recently, there was a preponderance of static populations of full-time employees working in fixed organizational structures. We are now seeing more varied combinations of full-time, part-time, and especially contracted workers within more fluid, umbrella-type corporate frameworks, including "**gig economy**" outfits such as Airbnb, TaskRabbit, and Managed by Q. The gig economy describes the prevailing environment where on-demand positions are common and many organizations contract with independent contractors for short-term engagements, often repeatedly.

The increasing numbers of individuals voluntarily working in **contingent and alternative-employment arrangements**—i.e., freelancers and consultants choosing not to be full-time, or even part-time, employees—are changing the employment equation for companies. Having more working-profile options for workers allows companies to be more responsive to fast-moving market conditions, while also giving many individuals new choices for their preferred work format. Ardent Partners' research revealed that 63 percent of employers are actually rethinking how enterprise work itself is addressed[98]—including who is going to complete the range of tasks. As part of that consideration, a more fluid working population at a company—including a greater number of workers who are not employees—creates a different dynamic for managers to handle, for maximizing engagement, productivity, and the benefits for the business.

Organizations that have an adaptable framework rather than a fixed structure can accommodate more flexible employment situations, as well as more dynamic market conditions. These types of corporate architectures are more frequently seen in new, gig-economy companies, where agility is seen as a critical core competence. However, a framework concept and construct can be utilized to enable much more flexibility in any type of organization. Evolution of the labor and employment laws is anticipated over time to create a new legal framework that accommodates the workforce evolution. However, for now, government data gathering and policies are currently lagging in their response to measure, track, and cater to the changes effectively.

Extending Talent Pools

As your company explores new markets, you may use freelancers and independent contractors to explore whether a particular direction will be beneficial to pursue or to test how you can address a new aspect of the market you are currently in. Different markets and approaches may need different types of people, and leveraging project-based and part-time talent can allow for effective experimentation. It can also be a low-risk scenario for your company and the **contingent worker** or independent contractor to try out a new relationship. Both parties can test the fit and situation—culture, attitude, skills, and more.

If a direction is proven to be worthwhile or necessary, then your company and the individual may mutually decide to agree on a longer-term role—whether employee-based, a project-by-project arrangement, or a continuing consulting contract. Your company now has more choices to consider for staffing up, depending on the results of the trials and on the interest of the worker to stay on longer, utilizing whatever particular type of employment arrangement suits both parties the most. As businesses expand and models adapt, so your workforce will likely ebb and flow and the configuration evolve.

It is beneficial to understand the forces behind the rise in freelancers and independent workers as stigmas associated with nonemployee situations fade and recognition of the benefits of this flexible workforce grows. When the Great Recession receded and the job market improved, of the millions of part-time workers surveyed, roughly half reported that they worked part time involuntarily. The other half were now choosing to work part time—even though full-time employment was again an option.[99]

As negative connotations associated with contract work decline, freelancing and consulting have become mainstream, with proactive and positive associations related to lifestyle choice and the ability to achieve the flexibility most workers are seeking. Independent contractors are also able to apply their skills across a broader variety of industry sectors and types of companies as the market accepts more diversified expert talent. This allows these individuals to have a greater variety of projects and spread their risk across a greater number of clients, resulting in a mutually beneficial skills-flexibility trade with the companies they work for.

Millions more people are choosing to work independently as Juno drivers, TaskRabbit errand runners, VetPronto vets, Axiom lawyers, a-connect consultants, and more. They want to apply themselves in targeted ways during the hours that suit them or doing the kinds of things they enjoy, where they can be most engaged. On the other side, your company can benefit by having a range of dedicated workers with the expertise you are looking for, as well as being able to take advantage of seasonal or project-based resources.

Many business models are changing with company-specific digital transformation as well as market evolution. The increasing availability of all types of contract workers gives your company a way to manage the uncertainty and associated risk. At the same time, the emerging desire for aligned values means that the cultural fit of all workers—long- and short-term, internal and external—becomes more important. Since bringing on new individuals or groups takes time and energy, companies are developing pools of familiar, culturally-aligned freelancers and consultants who may work on projects frequently over the course of a year or several years.

As the relationships deepen and extend, and temporary workers and independent contractors become included in more strategic, and even core, enterprise projects, employers who are paying more attention to the overall talent experience are including *all* workers. They are considering the experience of nonemployees as they communicate, interact, and work with employees and managers in accomplishing their tasks—how they are being hired, integrated, and supported—in order to engage them and promote high performance levels. Many organizations are looking to treat all workers in a similar manner and include nonemployees under human resources supervision rather than procurement.

These modifications are logical, as the broad pool of talent can include former employees as well as those who were previously prospective hires. This has long been customary practice in the advertising business, as well as with law firms, and is becoming more widespread across sectors. These workers are developing into an extension of the corporate community, and, indeed, members of this group may even become full- or part-time employees for periods of time, depending on particular circumstances. One media-agency chairman described their approach as an "accordion"—where the company swells and contracts depending on client needs and market conditions.

EMPLOYMENT CHOICES
AND COMBINATIONS

Are you looking for a full-time employee with a particular skill set and have already turned down several more experienced candidates, telling them "You are overqualified," and "We only have the budget to hire someone full-time with fewer years of experience"? If so, have you considered hiring the more seasoned prospect on a part-time basis with the budget that you have? You could benefit from their targeted expertise and mature management experience to get dedicated projects done efficiently in fewer hours. The person can also help nurture and train less-experienced employees in your organization and may be comfortable with a part-time role.

With a more dynamic definition of a company's workforce, the boundaries of the corporation are more "dotted"—or perhaps "perforated"—and less defined. Employees and contractors alike may work partly or wholly outside the company's offices, confirming the new reality that the "edges" of a company are no longer the walls of its office building. Indeed, there are a number of companies whose workers are totally dispersed, that have no central or even physical office at all. These firms are still able to create a sense of "the company" if they have a strong culture and values, which embrace and connect their corporate community, wherever their workers may be and however their employment is defined.

You can anticipate a more fluid workforce flowing in and out of your company as the contract-worker economy becomes even more accepted and supported and you are able to leverage key expert talent to suit longer- and shorter-term requirements. In certain industries, independent workers may have closely-connected clients, which might include some competitors, in a progressive, networked ecosystem where talented resources are "shared" within a sector. One engineer, for instance, recently explained to me that he worked for an engineering company for fifteen years in Europe. He then went to work for a very similar organization—a competitor to his previous employer—for eight years before moving back to the original firm. He commented that he knew a number of current and former colleagues who had taken similar career paths.

Going forward, there will be fewer, if any, monolithic corporations with clear and defined boundaries. Circumstances and careers will be much more fluid, with the majority of people taking on various combinations of full-time, part-time, and project roles as each of their sequential careers progress. Sometimes workers will be on the inside, and sometimes they will be part of an outer pool, transitioning back and forth at different times. Or they might only be in the outer pool, working for two or three companies at a time. Different, more adaptable operating constructs most easily accommodate different types of workers, and many organizations are exploring how this may best be achieved.

Frameworks Allowing Flexibility

Many existing organizational structures are legacies of the top-down, command-and-control era of corporate management. From financial institutions and retail empires to marketing agencies and manufacturing conglomerates, most of today's large organizations are staunchly hierarchical with distinct department and division silos and a structure that is very rigid and fixed by design.

In contrast, frameworks are conceptually more adaptable, while still giving form and stability. A corporate **framework** can create an umbrella under which people can work more flexibly, such as Uber, Handy, VetPronto, or TaskRabbit. A framework describes a canopy-type construct for a company where operational units are more integrated than before and may adapt over time, allowing for a flatter and/or more fluid hierarchy. The conceptual difference between a structure and a framework might best be explained by comparing a factory complex and an organic ecosystem. The latter has form and defined internal parts but with a natural fluidity, an understood progression over time, and inherent symbiotic relationships that the fixed building does not have. The natural ecosystem can therefore more easily accommodate different elements and combinations that may evolve.

Establishing a corporate framework does not mean daily or even weekly fluidity, nor does it signify transition to a form that enables adaptability but is devoid of rules or leadership. Instead, a company may first develop a conceptual framework that emphasizes and focuses on the talent and their interaction. Workers can navigate the organization more independently and fluidly rather than being separated by real or perceived structures and rigid boundaries. A framework enables integration between departments, allowing internal and external workers to communicate, collaborate, and contribute to projects more swiftly and efficiently on a temporary or longer-term basis.

So, the structural change here really has to do with adaptability within a fixed framework, while the fluidity should be thought of as a philosophical contrast to the rigidity of traditional organizational boundaries, which cordoned off people and teams. There will be little that is totally fixed as we progress. What is actually "fluid" has much more to do with the mindset, echoing a company culture that is open and accepting of change.

The benefit of this type of framework, in the conceptual sense, is that it can offer your company a form and an overall stability while still allowing more accommodation for elements and systems to transition. People can engage and perform best when they are comfortable, with understandable ways of operating and functional routines—but where there is also room for them to adapt and improve. Utilizing a framework concept, business operations can adapt while change is occurring, whether related to products, services, needs, or the workforce within an office building. Frameworks can permit and support very different business models to accomplish many goals, accommodate projects coming together on a temporal basis, facilitate integration between departments, and allow more responsive reactions to market changes.

A framework is also preferable in enabling workplace flexibility. More flexibility allows workers options to create the working circumstances they want or need—whether it is more autonomy, more time at home, better ways to collaborate and contribute, or just improved well-being overall. However, this does not mean a fluid workplace. When workplace flexibility is mentioned, many people think it means fluidity and an unmanageable and chaotic working dynamic. Flexibility also is not synonymous with working from home.

There are many flexible models, and the on-demand or real-time option is only one of them. Workplace flexibility can still mean fixed, but different, hours or be solely office-based. For example, one employee might choose a compressed workweek, where they are still working a forty-hour week in the office—just ten hours a day, four days a week. Another employee could choose a different flexible-hours model in which they work an eight-hour day and five-day workweek, just starting at 11 o'clock a.m. and finishing at 7 o'clock p.m. These are both common flexible models, where the "flexibility" in the worker's schedule is fixed on a weekly basis. The flexibility is about changing the employee's schedule to something that is other than the traditional 9 a.m. to 5 p.m., Monday through Friday workweek.

Leveraging the framework format, gig-economy companies provide an umbrella organization under which a large percentage of workers have the ability to choose the times they want to work and even how many hours. These can be advantageous conditions for those individuals who would like to work independently but prefer not to do the sales and marketing to get the clients they serve or projects they work on. In many situations, it is the umbrella company that finds the customers and connects them with the independent contractors working within the framework, who service them on demand. However, some of these new framework-enabled work models represent such a departure from traditional employment arrangements that government regulation is not yet equipped to track and deal with them comprehensively.

Employment Equation Evolution

In the effort to understand and improve work environments, one prevailing issue is a lack of reliable numbers to monitor the changes that are in progress. The Bureau of Labor Statistics (BLS) has yet to update its means of gathering data in a way that measures some pivotal aspects affecting the evolving workplace. For example, if a freelance worker has been surveyed during a week when he or she is not working or does not have a project, the BLS often counts that person as unemployed. True comprehension of new, more fluid working situations will be enabled by the reporting of more accurate

freelancer and employment numbers overall, after thoughtful modification of periodic-survey questions.

These matter all the more because the health of the U.S. economy
is interpreted each month, partially based on the much-anticipated
employment statistics. Countless decisions are based on this data—
not just related to short-term stock-market transactions but also
important government policies. These include determinations about
labor and employment laws, health care, and pension plans, as well as
Federal Reserve policies that decide on financial liquidity and small
businesses' ability to get credit.

The contributions and needs of this expanding, significant
"contingent- and alternative-working arrangement" segment of the
labor force are important to include in development of strategies and
decisions relating to government policies. These encompass high-level
goals, such as reaching "full employment," a scenario where every
"eligible worker is fully employed." When first defined in Keynesian
times, this essentially meant able-bodied male workers working full
time. Now, however, eligible workers obviously encompass a much
larger and varied band of the population and may feel fully-employed
working fewer than forty hours per week.

Therefore, it is important for the government to understand
the new composition of the labor force and its modified combination of profiles in order to make progress and formulate updated,
appropriate labor-market- and employment-related objectives and
policies. The appropriate associated strategies and tactics can then be
developed with relevant impact for large and small companies and
the contingent workers and independent contractors (for specific
definitions, please consult the lexicon) who work for and with them.
For example, one outcome of the Affordable Care Act was to separate
health coverage from full-time jobs. This was beneficial in enabling

those who were unable or chose not to obtain full-time work to get health-insurance coverage while they served their client(s) with their expertise.

However, as laws are amended and new laws introduced, many elements are needed to create a fully-functioning regulatory framework to facilitate and support nonemployee workers as a core pillar of the future labor force. It has been increasingly evident that government policies are ready for revision to provide support in matters such as specific worker protection, health care, and retirement. These elements are important to ensure that the flexibility and availability of a large independent workforce works for all parties. Health-care-related law modifications will hopefully include appropriate provisions and options for nonemployees going forward. Other gaps are expected to be filled over time to support the swelling independent workforce as an equal opportunity alongside other employment options.

Another issue is that there are currently two key designations ascribed by U.S. labor and employment laws—traditional employees and independent contractors. These do not appear sufficient to cover the needs and nuances of the new working models with associated benefits and protection. This has become especially evident with the rise of the gig economy and numerous desired and increasingly prevalent flexible-work options.

While there have been close to twenty elements that define someone as an employee rather than a contractor, under prevailing laws, the "control"—or "actionable choices"—that people have over their work situation and how and when they are managing their project work or tasks are core determinants. However, it is the very distribution of choice, and who has what degree of control, that is in transition. Control—or the ability to make certain decisions or actionable choices—is moving along the continuum from the employer toward the employee. As noted earlier, new choices may include location and the number and times of working hours.

Such choices were key points of contention in the highly-publicized class-action lawsuit against Uber that launched in 2013 in California. Who now has what control when it comes to the employer and the worker? Are Uber's drivers actually employees rather than independent contractors? As control shifts, what does that mean for Uber and many similar umbrella-type organizations that enable the flexible work models of their extended workforce? While the case was ultimately settled, the legal outcome is not my focus, despite the challenge of making a ruling in evidently evolving circumstances. My purpose is to highlight that the main conclusion of many observing the progress and outcome of the lawsuit was that twentieth-century labor and employment laws need to be updated to accommodate the new types of working models in the twenty-first century.

As one possible solution, in December 2015, the Hamilton Project[100] published a proposal to create a new category of worker called the "independent worker." This category would be positioned between an employee (who uses a W-2 form when filing with the IRS) and an independent contractor (who uses a 1099 form). This new worker class would enable businesses to "provide benefits and protections that employees currently receive without fully assuming the legal costs and risks of becoming an employer. Such benefits and protections include the freedom to organize and collectively bargain, the ability to pool (eg, a suite of employer-provided benefits such as health insurance and retirement accounts; income and payroll tax withholding), civil-rights protections, and an opt-in program for workers' compensation insurance."[101]

This is a well-thought-through and serious proposition, with an advisory council that lists heavyweights spanning corporate America, from General Atlantic to Google; major private-equity shops and banking groups, from Warburg Pincus and the Carlyle Group to Evercore and Citigroup; and high-level economists, public-policy professors, and former policymakers, from Tim Geithner to Bob Rubin and Larry Summers. It is only one idea. It would require revision of a number of existing laws as well as much debate and modification before being a viable possibility. Whether derived from this proposal or another, some middle-ground solution is expected, unless the private sector acts first.

The modernization of the current U.S. employment and labor laws will seek to redefine who does and does not work for your company and how each type of worker is required to be paid, supported, and protected. Revision will not happen quickly. However, it is worth monitoring developments in this area, as they could dramatically affect your future costs, obligations, and hiring strategies.

Chapter 9: Takeaways

- **First Principles**: Contemplate the optimal way for work to be accomplished for your business and by whom, recognizing the different tasks, skills, and people needed. Consider leveraging the external pool of nonemployee workers, which has much greater depth and range now, including those who are well-aligned with your company's culture and mindset. Study the benefits of a more flexible corporate construct, such as a framework concept, to allow for greater organizational adaptability and responsiveness. Reflect on the definition of "your company" and its boundaries and who is or might be part of the extended corporate community.

- **Priorities**:

  ▫ Engagement—Cultural fit is important for engaging nonemployee workers. Developing a pool of familiar freelancers and independent contractors that your company works with on a reasonably regular basis can be a win-win for everyone.

  ▫ Personalization—It is beneficial to consider how to support all your workers, including freelancers and contract workers, so they can perform well. Having all workers overseen by human resources is a new development as use of contractors increases, promoting more equity of treatment across your workforce.

  ▫ Integration—Time is often wasted if independent contractors are not able to work seamlessly with employees, such as being able to connect easily into the corporate network to share files or print. It is beneficial to ensure different worker groups are supported and integrated to the greatest extent possible, while allowing for security and other concerns. A corporate framework permits greater integration, decreasing intracompany boundaries, and so enables a more flexible and agile response to changing market needs.

  ▫ Choice—The greater selection of targeted nonemployee talent can allow for a more stable employee workforce, leveraging experts and particular skill sets as and when needed.

- **Evaluation**:

  ▫ How many former employees do occasional work for your company?

- ▫ Does your company frequently use contractors to supply skill sets that specific projects or operations need?

- ▫ Do you already engage some freelancers who work regularly with specific people or departments at your company?

- ▫ How many nonemployees are considered part of your extended corporate community?

- ▫ Do you keep in touch with them at regular intervals?

- ▫ Does your corporate structure easily allow for agile and flexible working models?

- ▫ Are you satisfied with your company's ability to be responsive to market changes and/or new customer requests?

- ▫ How much do division and department members talk to each other and share information about their projects?

- ▫ How rigid is the separation—physical, psychological, and social—between the departments in your company?

- **Metrics**: Examples include: Increase in number of freelancers and consultants used during a typical quarter; increase in speed of response to customer demands; increase in number of teams working across departments and divisions; decrease in setup time for a nonemployee starting work on a company project; increase of information flow and sharing of ideas across divisions; and rise in number of people considered part of the corporate community who have worked on company projects.

CHAPTER 10

CURRENT CONUNDRUMS: CHOICE AND CONTEXT

If you could design the perfect job for yourself, what would it look like?

Almost every one of the hundreds of people I have put this question to over the last six years have responded with a blank look, raised eyebrows, and a shrug. (Try it and see.) Actually, this is to be expected.

The emerging corporate landscape offers an unprecedented plethora of working models that is generating consternation and confusion—among executives, team leaders, and team members alike. This is completely understandable. While the objective of offering more choice to workers is to increase their engagement, creating options for personalization also involves the participation of each individual in making new selections. Supporting your workforce in navigating the new possibilities and evolving landscape will reduce concern and bewilderment and accelerate and increase the many benefits that may be enjoyed.

In parallel, the multigenerational workforce brings a new mix of mindsets, needs, and desires in their virtual and physical, remote and proximate work environments. Assumption checking is essential to promote connection, create common context, and avoid misunderstanding and misaligned expectations. It is important to establish clear project criteria, expectations, processes, and milestones.

Being Challenged by Choice

What's so hard about choice? To be worthwhile, making choices requires thought and attention. It takes a process and some time to make important decisions. So, the current challenge is that the majority of people facing the new range of working options either are not used to having many work-related alternatives or do not have much relevant experience to help them make their choices. Without appropriate attention paid by the person or people involved, the process is often superficial and the results therefore suboptimal—for all concerned.

Baby Boomer and older Generation X employees typically started and developed their careers during a period when the linear, continuous, and compounding career path was the norm and the expectation. Movement—either to another company or even another department internally—was discouraged and often viewed suspiciously. So changes were typically minimal over the course of someone's working life. Many did end up working for just one company, and even one division, all of their working career, while others may have made a couple of thoughtful choices at critical junctures. During that period, an individual's job was clearly defined and constrained in scope, and for most people the work was done at the office, five days a week, between the hours of 9 o'clock a.m. and 5 o'clock p.m. at a minimum. Options related to one's working profile—when and where the work was done and what it comprised—were generally few and far between. That was it.

Now the situation could not be more different. "Permanent" (read career-long) full-time jobs do not exist anymore. Linear careers have been replaced by less-defined, and more-**latticed**, networked, and diversified ones. The Great Recession also played a role in changing the job market for good—starting with millions experiencing or witnessing the loss of full-time employment, then scrambling to get whatever work possible—whether part time, consulting, or freelance projects.

These solutions became longer term than most imagined and so prevalent that stigma associated with non-full-time work decreased. In parallel, technological advances changed the game as easily accessible software platforms and powerful online and networked applications affordably facilitated project-and independent-work formats. With greater acceptance and technical support, working paradigms that included much more flexibility were enjoyed and took on new significance.

Within organizations, corporate employees armed with similarly powerful technology are now each looking to develop a personalized working profile—the outline of a customized job situation. Their desire is to create a profile that is more suited to their specific combination of circumstances, relevant for them alone and a better fit for all their activities, corporate and noncorporate. However, it is a challenge for each person to understand and make good choices and work out how to design the right profile for themselves if they have not done it before—and very few people have. They have to be able to work out how to prioritize their activities effectively *and* how to fit in which activities where appropriate.

"Now THIS is a great way to coordinate our flex schedules!"

As all employees consider their possibilities, the implicit or explicit understanding that they become personally responsible for the choices they make increases the stakes dramatically. It is simpler, and often "easier," to struggle against someone else's direction and decisions than to make and then possibly be dissatisfied with one's own choices. As employees gain more control over the format of their jobs, so do they have to be more accountable for their choices.

At the same time, few employees have previously had the need or occasion to actively be self-aware in the workplace with regard to how they work best, or even what they really like doing or perform best at. Without help, as noted in chapter 6, it is therefore hard for most employees to embark on the involved process of recognizing their strengths, understanding their options fully, evaluating their situations, and prioritizing their needs in order to make choices they can be comfortable with in the future. During the process, they realize they have to take full responsibility for the conclusions they arrive at.

In developing their optimal working profile, employees consider at least three core aspects—their strengths, working styles, and overall situation. Focused and relevant training to navigate the process can help employees arrive at effective decisions much more easily and quickly and will yield greater benefits for all parties. Coaching can be delivered through a combination of videos, workshops, and mentoring, while guidance can be provided to support the process, including useful tools as mentioned in chapter 1.

First of all, the goal is to focus on leveraging individuals' strengths, as they will likely do better and enjoy work more if they are good at it. The consensus is moving away from the idea that management should help employees make up for their weaknesses, instead seeking ways to fill in for one employee's weaknesses with another one's strengths or to leverage other resources. The emphasis is now to augment employees' strengths instead. As also mentioned in chapter 6, StrengthsFinder is helpful in identifying a person's strengths.[102]

Second, in terms of working style, *how* do employees work best? Do they perform better when they work independently, or do they thrive in a group environment? Would they feel isolated working from home? Are they focused and disciplined when not being actively supervised (which could be office based or remote)? Are they most productive early or later in the morning, or are they more effective working late in the evening? Will they be able to set the boundaries necessary to work productively in the new environment of their choice?

The answers to all these questions are important in determining when and where a person may be most engaged and productive. Myers-Briggs and Harrison Assessments are effective tests that can surface and clarify individual personality traits and characteristics, including how different individual types may interact in pairs and groups. To give additional support in the process, Myers-Briggs also proffers types of jobs and roles that could be well-suited for specific personality types. This can be useful for aligning someone in a more suitable job, if some role adaptation is anticipated or desired relating to strengths highlighted in the first step.

Third, what timing and location would be appropriate based on these factors, considered in combination with other team members' profiles *and* their own noncorporate obligations, as well as the needs of their family and others? What formula of hours and days would work best to serve their team, completion of their work, and the rest of their activities? Could it be 9 a.m. to 5 p.m., five days a week, working from home two days? Or would a profile be preferable with the employee working five days a week in the office, just starting and leaving much earlier?

The outcome of the exercise—when an employee has a customized job and work format—has been repeatedly shown to decrease distractions, reduce stress, and improve health and happiness, leading to increased productivity.[103] At the same time, as explained earlier, the employer's very act of making the effort to understand a person's desires, needs, and sensibilities earns much respect and trust in return. This helps enhance the connection between that employee with their employer, and thence engagement typically increases as well. Moreover, there is a greater overall loyalty to a company that implements the personalized job profile. A significant added benefit is gained in helping each employee customize their work profile, as both parties better understand that person's strengths and working style, leading to improved management interactions and more effective performance.

It can be worthwhile to make employees aware that no decision is final. The workdays made boundaryless by technology can also be challenging to define appropriately in a new context, leading to certain modifications resulting from experimentation. New configurations are best confirmed through trials using metrics that are relevant for new working models, to determine if a person has chosen the optimal work setup. In addition, reassessments are also advisable after whatever period your company determines is appropriate, which can be communicated at the beginning of the process. Then employees can also see that the company understands the dynamic reality of their work and lives overall.

However, management or employee fear and inertia can be major hindrances to starting and completing this process effectively. These are the core reasons that so many worthwhile initiatives do not happen or are not accomplished well. As mentioned in the introduction, not moving forward—not using learnings to achieve progress— is also a choice. Stagnation *is* an option and, to some, it may actually seem easier at first glance. So while you push for progress, many within your organization may well not *want* to advance. Research provided throughout this book will support your ability to communicate that inaction will also have dire consequences in today's business environment. Your company's future ability to hire, engage, and keep the leaders, creative thinkers, strong technologists, and others that it needs now and going forward, especially younger hires, will be determined by efforts made to engage your workforce and by the personalized choices they are offered.

Despite the energy and attention required to support and coach your employees in developing their personalized work situations, the engagement and ensuing productivity rewards for your company are numerous. Inertia in a large corporation is obviously substantial, just remembering the physics: an inert object requires "external force" to get it moving, creating momentum—mass times velocity. The larger the object, the more difficult that is, as greater force needs to be exerted. However, in this case, a positive perspective is that when the intention to advance is activated, forward motion is more easily sustained, because there are multiple forces at work. Technology developments, the evolving marketplace, and workers' new demands are just a few of the motivating powers that will aid your efforts and propel your company's progress.

Once the decision to act has been made, it is important to share it with the whole company so that it can be understood completely; then executives and employees alike are aware of the future path that the organization is taking and why. Each person can be fully on board and involved in the process, making the transition as efficient and effective as possible—for themselves individually, their teams, managers, leaders, and the company as a whole.

To make the best use of newly-available choices, leaders can review all the different areas affected. Additional options can be offered to employees to support their engagement, sharing new aspects of control relating to business processes, collaboration, operational matters, or the employment framework in general. Encouraging your workers to take responsibility for more choices can play an important role in engaging them, where they become more involved in and take more ownership of the development, process, and results.

Communicating with Context

Context is another area of confusion and challenge. Context is critical. So many workplace interactions are rife with misinterpretations, judgments, polarizing opinions, and unhelpful labels. Intergenerational misunderstandings and communications at cross purposes are at the core of many of the current unproductive exchanges and negative experiences.

(Mis)understanding context can result in one person describing another as "entitled" instead of "enlightened," or as having a "poor work ethic" instead of a "balanced approach to work." Misaligned context can have both parties in a discussion feeling disrespected, seemingly undervaluing each other's expertise.

How or why does this happen? Most people believe or feel that their own context is "the truth" and that their own understanding and interpretations, usually built from their personal experiences and history, are the correct ones. This seems particularly applicable in business situations, which may appear more "normalized" and straightforward, with less of the character-driven drama and emotion of family- and friend-related experiences and stories.

However, the reality and context of each person is unique, and those of identifiable groups, as large as generations, can differ greatly because of the diverging experiences they have of the same external circumstances. An important example is how Baby Boomers (born between 1946 and 1964), Generation Xers (born between 1965 and 1979), and Millennials (born between 1980 and 1995) are all and each reacting to the post–Great Recession transformation of the workplace.

As discussed in chapter 3, every person is an individual first and may also identify with one or more relevant groups. Many from each generation do not identify with, or feel similar to, the stereotypes of their generation, since their own experiences may vary greatly from those of the generational group and have many more similarities with those of another generation or a different group entirely. What follows are broad illustrative examples.

Tom Turner is a typical Baby Boomer. He is currently winding down his career but is interested in staying mentally active and in continuing to earn at a reduced level, so as not to deplete his retirement funds too soon. He is looking to decrease his workload and core responsibilities but would like to stay involved and participate in the labor force, as well as have more leisure time. He is very much aligned with the increasing use of independent workers, as he can leverage his own expertise in targeted ways. Turner is also comfortable with the new diversification of careers, because he benefits from it, able to transition his career and apply his skills in different areas. After many years in the job market, Turner is now looking for more purpose and alignment with his values in the jobs and projects he engages in, more so than he did in earlier corporate roles.

Generation Xers, in contrast, are mostly in their prime revenue-generating years. Jessica Simmons is one of them. She has certainly had her own post-forty "epiphany" about the meaning of life, and she desires to create a reasonable balance between work and her other activities, including time with her family. At the same time, she is keenly aware of her career arc and relative positioning and is interested in maximizing, or at least optimizing, her income to build up her nest egg for the future.

Simmons exhibits general Generation X-type interest in greater opportunities for workplace flexibility and expresses the usual apprehension about possible trade-offs or penalties, whether real or perceived. The decreased job security that accompanies the changing career dynamics is perhaps the most concerning to her, based on her need to create and consolidate financial security. Simmons has not been accustomed to the incorporation of purpose in the corporate environment during her career thus far. Instead, she is involved in nonprofit and social-impact activities that fulfill her desires in these areas through personal channels running in parallel with her profession.

Mike Jones is a Millennial, with yet another set of reactions. The current set of circumstances IS his inherent reality, so his natural approach is to absorb it, seek to understand it, and find out how best to make it work for him. He joined the workforce during the period of recovery from the Great Recession, and one consequence is that he is risk-averse. This does not necessarily mean he would never quit a job without having another one lined up, but he avoids taking on the long-term responsibility of buying a home or car, because he does not want to take on major financial obligations in an unstable economy where long-term, secure full-time jobs are few and far between.

Jones is eager to develop his potential and succeed, where success is defined more by a combination of work-related achievements and the wealth of his experiences than by the physical assets he is able to amass. He is more focused on the present than on future gains and is interested in creating a balanced role for work that is integrated with the rest of his life. Just like Millennials Stoker and Coburn in chapter 3, Jones sees "hard work" as doing something he enjoys, and it is more about the intensity of effort that he applies and the results he achieves than the hours he works. He also cares very much about the values of any organization he works for. His employer's and his own contributions towards achieving the company's purpose are critical to Jones's motivation, similar to Baby Boomer Turner's desire to have purpose in the work he does. Also like Turner, Jones is well-aligned with the diversified career model—however, for him, it is the only one he really knows!

The work context for each of these individuals is different in some aspects and similar in others, all of which in combination determines the frame of reference and each individual's approach. It is the contrasts and diversity of understanding that affect interpretations of and consequent reactions to a discussion, request, scenario, or task. An individual from any of the generations may certainly give responses that differ enormously from some or all of those described above based on their own particular experiences. The point is that anyone can have a very different appreciation of a situation or work issue based on their own history, circumstances, and contexts. No one is right or wrong. However, a useful and productive approach is to try to understand any different reaction from the other person's perspective rather than one's own point of view, without judgment.

A great example of different contexts leading to dissimilar approaches was highlighted by a lecturer teaching a class of Millennial students. He challenged the group to find out his birthday, with a prize for whomsoever discovered it first, and then he walked out of the room. Everyone used their phone or laptop to search for the answer, and not one single person went out to ask him in person.[104] What is the norm to one person may be lateral thinking to another, and each brings a different perspective and ideas.

People who have grown up with a self-reliant approach, able to ask their smartphone for the answer to any question, may be less likely to ask questions of the people around them. However, the subtleties and nuances of many situations or answers are not necessarily captured or easily surfaced online or conveyed digitally—summarized in video or audio bites or bullet points. As a result, many subtle but important information gaps may exist that might not emerge until a misunderstanding or difference in expectations has resulted. Other contextual miscommunication may ensue from dissimilar interpretations of data or unintended use of incomplete data.

Deliberately creating a common context at the beginning of a project or new situation by sharing assumptions allows a first-principles type approach in setting a neutral ground of understanding between people or among members of a group. Gaps in knowledge or in relevant experience may then be revealed in an impartial and dispassionate way. Proactive questioning can help in discovering any discrepancies in understanding and achieve alignment—over-communicating at the outset, until each party is well understood by the other(s).

Processes do not need to be dictated. Instead, sharing and refining parameters together can best engage all parties involved, allowing them to contribute and incorporate their personal perspectives, with an outcome that is integrated and agreed on. Cross-generational interactions and cooperation—including formal and informal mentoring pairs—can help bridge experience gaps. These may often involve technology-related matters and those derived from expertise built over time, so useful bidirectional sharing of knowledge can be very fruitful, as can encouraging group activities and exchanges to build cross-discipline and intra/inter-team relationships.

With a new array of choices and contexts, it would be a Herculean task to create the perfect job for each of your employees—even if they knew what that looked like! A key objective is to engage your workers, and that includes giving them new work choices and assisting them in discovering and refining a personalized working profile. Their new work situation can then be customized to the extent possible, depending on all team members' strengths and circumstances, as well as the needs of the business. The process of developing that profile involves each individual's committed participation and a sharing of personal context, which deepens the employer/employee relationship and helps build respect and trust. This greater connection also benefits communication and collaboration, smoothing over—or at least generating some slack—when there are context-based misunderstandings! Other miscommunications can be reduced through a purposeful approach to sharing assumptions and creating common ground that values and integrates all parties' perspectives.

Chapter 10 Takeaways

- **First Principles**: Reflect on how employees can be supported to make good decisions in areas where they are not accustomed to having options or have little experience to draw on. Think through how they can optimize their working profiles based on their personality, strengths, individual tasks, work style, and combination of work, life activities, and obligations. Contemplate how to promote the sharing of assumptions in order to set common ground between employees and combinations of workers, as well as vendors, partners, and customers. Consider the benefits of bidirectional mentoring programs and cross-generational teams to enhance sharing of expertise and experience.

- **Priorities**:

   □ Engagement—Choice is a critical component of the Future-of-Work environment for engaging workers and giving them more control over their work and working situations. However, without guidance, choice can cause confusion.

▫ Personalization—With direction about the newly-available choices, employees can make decisions that are relevant for them as individuals. They can prioritize their activities and obligations appropriately, and as a result, numerous benefits can accrue to both employer and employees.

▫ Integration—As more options are shared, employees are also recognizing other team members' needs and coordinating and compromising with them to optimize outcomes for the team as a whole. Team members, as well as cross-generational and other inclusive groups, are brought closer through integrated schedules as well as initiatives to increase communication and knowledge-sharing.

▫ Choice—Employees are being given greater ability to control aspects of their jobs and working profiles, which can be seen as a shift along the employer/employee continuum towards the employee. This a central theme in the Future-of-Work changes, with the resulting higher engagement and improved productivity.

- **Evaluation**:

  ▫ How extensively have workplace-flexibility policies been communicated and implemented at your company?

  ▫ How many employees have taken advantage of workflex arrangements?

  ▫ What percentage of employees have personalized their working profile?

  ▫ Are employees given detailed choices that can be personalized for their working profiles, before they coordinate with other team members' working profiles?

- What kind of coaching is given to employees to help them determine the appropriate flexible model or personalized working profile for themselves?

- How well are different generations and divisions integrated across the company in teams and other groups?

- Are there formal or informal mentoring programs at your company? How many employees are involved in mentoring-program pairs?

- **Metrics**: Examples include: Increase in number of choices offered to employees relating to workplace-flexibility policies; increase in percentage of employees leveraging workplace flexibility; increase in hours of coaching provided to employees to support their decision-making in development of new, personalized work arrangements; increase in number of teams with cross-generational members; increase in number of active mentoring pairs; increase in workers' sense of cohesion and proactive cooperation across generations and division; and increase in the number of hours of communications training to support context setting and sharing.

CHAPTER 11

CAREERS: MAPPING AND MENTORING

The "linear, continuous, compounding career" is over.

NEW CAREER PARADIGM: INCOME, NOT JOBS.

I sneaked that first statement into an earlier chapter—it may not have registered, but we all know it's true. Earlier this year, someone said to me, "It's not over *yet* … but, yes, it will be soon." In that case, I pointed out, by definition it *is* already over. There are no more lifelong or thirty-year careers at one company, and I predict that even a decade at the same organization will be an anomaly in the future.

This new career paradigm is more involved, for everyone— employers, employees, and independent workers alike. Younger recruits are looking for guidance to navigate these uncharted waters. At a DisruptHR gathering in New York in 2016, a Millennial presenter announced, "We are looking for a 'mentoring culture.'" However, younger workers are not the only ones needing direction in understanding how careers are changing and what to do for their own personal career development, or what the next steps are now that the linear, continuous, and compounding career is no longer an option.

A confluence of forces has resulted in nascent career paradigms that are very different—with unprecedented diversity, discontinuity, sector changes, lateral moves, and multiple transitions. For individuals, the emphasis is moving to revenue generation, not jobs. For corporations, careers are becoming individualized and latticed. Subsequent positions for an individual employee may now involve a sideways or diagonal move rather than a vertical move straight up the corporate ladder in the same area.

As a result, the concept of **career-experience management** can be adopted to encompass your employees' new working profiles, as well as to create and map their evolving career prospects and develop plans. With an unfamiliar landscape to consider, creating a **mentoring culture** can provide beneficial internal support for employees throughout your organization. The inputs of employees themselves, in writing their own **personal business plans,** can also be enlisted directly to help determine their career plans. New types of careers are also reflected in the resumes of prospective hires. It is useful to be able to interpret these appropriately in the new environment as the evolving career dynamics affect your recruiting approach and needs.

Emerging Career Paradigms

There are many factors contributing to the changing career trajectories, including: the demise of the patriarchal organization; ubiquitous connectivity increasing competitive pressures; the change in emphasis from value creation based on hard assets to that based on intangible ones, such as people and intellectual property;[105] the fast growth of nonroutine tasks, including project work;[106] technology advances resulting in shifting business models; associated staffing needs evolving in terms of roles, numbers of people, and skills; and the increased size of the voluntary and available independent-contractor workforce.

Furthermore, the traditional linear, fixed career paths have been suboptimal for many people. Those paths assumed conformity. The emphasis on continuity neither acknowledged societal developments nor accommodated any hiatus in employment—to take care of children or an ailing relative, for example, or for any other needs or pursuits. The two-dimensional, linear aspect did not allow for exploratory lateral moves or changing gears—especially for workers who realized they had not made the right choice at the beginning of their career. Further education—whether business school or another type of course or additional certification—had been the key accepted way for someone to change track in midcareer. However, this often has not been an accessible or viable option—whether time- and or cost-related—for making a transition to another area or discipline.

"Permanent," full-time jobs are over. They have been for a while, but we haven't really wanted to admit it to ourselves. We are now beginning to see what is generally replacing them—full-time jobs are expected to come and go over the course of longer lifetimes and many careers. In parallel and in sequence will be periods of part-time work, freelance projects, and longer-term consulting work—for the majority of us, not just a small segment of the working population.

"Every worker needs to 'shed' old
habits. You'll do well."

For instance, a typical twenty-nine-year-old man will often have had multiple work experiences, including much project work and/or temporary positions, probably working at both start-ups and larger corporations. When he finds a discipline he really enjoys or a mission he is passionate about at a company he has a strong cultural fit with, then a longer tenure is possible, especially if he is offered opportunities to develop his potential and move around within the organization. He foresees a succession of careers, some of which may be related, others going off in new directions, mostly leveraging the same strengths. He will have future jobs that include part-time roles, additional project work for one or multiple clients, and certain full-time stints, some of which last longer than others. He will keep learning and getting training throughout his career, taking courses and/or getting new certifications. He will save money to cover future periods of low income but doesn't think about retirement much as a concept.

A characteristic career evolution for a forty-seven-year-old woman will have many similarities to that of the twenty-nine-year-old. However, she will have to transition to a diversified career model—possibly after more than twenty years working at just one or two large corporations (at whatever level of seniority). She may well not have been working in an area that she enjoyed very much and may desire first to explore her particular strengths and discover which fields and companies she is most interested in. She will take some time to acclimate to a new "self-centered," revenue-focused model going forward, relying on a variety of employment arrangements and job and project opportunities. She will apply her expertise in different ways, re-skilling when desired or necessary to move across sectors and change the scope and application of her capabilities. She will likely also have other related and distinct careers, accompanied by ongoing learning, prior to a delayed or phased period of retirement in the future, depending on what pension she has been able to amass previously.

With all these changes, people are experiencing their careers very differently. Previously, someone's identity was company-centric or had a strong and long-term corporate allegiance. A man might consider himself an "AT&T guy" after more than twenty years working there and would not be planning to move. However, identity is now more individual-centric—with more weighting on someone's personal "brand" or story and proactive career self-management. Tenure at any specific company may not be extended for years, and revenue will often come from more than one source at the same time.

People's recognition of the new reality often depends on their current work situation. Once employees are attuned to new career scenarios, it is very likely to affect their relationship with the company they are working for and their engagement in their work, through no fault or ill-intent of the organization. The employees are just acknowledging the reality of the current employment equation and their "actual" bond with the organization they work for. Employers that are transparent about employment situations with their workers are able to develop trust-based relationships founded on realistic dialog. It is not about guaranteeing anything but being clear and authentic.

For example, Rob Newton feels unsettled. He is employed at a large corporation with a relatively high turnover where there was a round of layoffs recently. He has noticed increasing use of independent contractors. He has also become aware of the more transient and varied nature of new career profiles from chatting with former colleagues, as well as from discussions with consultants. He has developed a new understanding of the range of possibilities and probabilities for his own career. He is considering what his prospects are at his current employer and is thinking hard about what else he might do elsewhere over the longer term. Newton is interested in staying at the company, but they haven't yet talked to him about his future prospects at all, and he doesn't want to be blindsided by any reorganization or layoffs. So, he is actively working on the next steps of his own career plan, looking at the realistic possibilities where he is working now as well as what else he might want to do in the future and for whom. If Newton's current employer wants to keep him for the longer term or even the medium term, they would be wise to have an open and interactive discussion with him about the next steps of his career there.

For many corporate employees, the career fragmentation and onus on individuals to be more involved in a less straightforward career plan can feel like a radical change from previous circumstances. I have had conversations with many employees of corporations who are concerned about perceived—or real—increased job instability. They are also anxious about how to start and how to drive ongoing proactive participation in their career planning and may be distracted from their work while they get accustomed to the new circumstances. Hundreds of people I have spoken with are already working out how to evaluate their current and future situations, as well as how to plan as necessary to reduce risk and be assured of as steady revenue streams and employment situations as possible going forward.

At the same time, the demise of the traditional corporate career track has left quite a vacuum in its place. It is implicitly understood by executives, managers, and new recruits alike that compounding job progression and long-term, discipline-specific career trajectories are not to be expected. However, for the most part that has not been acknowledged explicitly, nor has much been done to create "Careers 2.0" scenarios. All too often, nothing new has been proposed, leading to employees' bewilderment, disappointment, frustration, and, in the worst cases, departure. This has been a frequent catalyst of, or at least a significant contributor to, turnover for younger recruits.

In the past, fresh hires were able to "jump" onto a relevant career track at their new company, without any real guidance necessary. Human resources focused on the top ten percent—the "Hi-Pos," or high potentials—and nurtured them, destined for future leadership roles. However, in current situations, where the strategic and tactical scope of HR's responsibilities has not yet expanded, a new recruit can easily arrive, recognize the absence of any discernible pathways, and flounder when he or she receives little or no direction. As the nature and format of careers transition, a person can easily be lost in the confusion, feel disoriented and disconnected from the new employer, and leave.

Managing the Career Experience

The corporate-career realm is ripe for significant innovation—with more participation anticipated from both the employer and the employee in a more relationship-driven world. In a tighter labor market, with a focus on the talent agenda, the emphasis for employers seems to be shifting to "career-experience management," as coined for me by Nathan Knight, a strategic thinker in talent and organizational development at a major media and entertainment company.

Knight's forward-thinking concepts in development regarding careers and career-experience management include recording elements of prospective hires' future career development in their employment contracts. In conversation with me, he explained, "For employees with contracts—this is an explicit negotiation. For those who value development—particularly in a world where time seems more precious than ever and the trade-off of limiting yourself versus job security is not what it once was—this becomes a way to make the value of staying more tangible and the prospect of growth more real. For employees without contracts—taking a similar approach to the job-offer process, with development plans that have activities, costs and timelines spelled out and agreed upon by both sides, could be a differentiator when deciding between offers or staying where they are."

Discussion between the employer and potential employee that takes place during the hiring process can positively influence prospective hires' decision-making and later on-boarding experience as well as their understanding of how their career will be handled. Prospective employees then will have clarity about their potential and future roles at the company—letting them know that some career projection has already been thought through and planned for. Most importantly, they can recognize at the outset the commitment that their new employer has to their future, and, as Knight describes, "they are involved in crafting that future and determining the value of the company's support from their perspective."

An employee's involvement in their work is a central driver of the new work philosophies and practices, and career development is another important aspect. A lack of any career-planning discussion can be detrimental to the continued engagement of an employee, while proactive interaction about it can be helpful for stimulating that employee's participation in their work and interest in prolonging a relationship with the organization.

New, latticed careers are emerging that include lateral and diagonal transitions as well as the traditional vertical path and are more flexible and adaptable, which works both for the employee and the employer. So, a new step for the career of someone like Newton might be to move within or across a division or department and be rotated to a very different position or area, especially since he is not that senior yet. Newton's future career progression might incorporate a sequence of roles that are additive experiences, even if not promoting him immediately to a more senior position. This "circulation" helps sustain his interest with new tasks, broadens his skill set (benefiting his current and future careers), and gives him an understanding of additional areas of the organization to leverage in the future. Through investing time and effort in training Newton as he learns new responsibilities and capabilities, the company develops him as a more rounded executive who has greater knowledge of different units, teams, and operations across the business.

Taking a first-principles approach and stepping back, it actually benefits your organization not to have workers as limited to one discipline as they used to be. As needs change and customers have new and different demands, adaptability is now essential for the survival and success of your business. A more flexible mentality and a broader knowledge and experience base will help your employees be successful in a workplace that is in transition and will also support and enhance the growth of your business in an uncertain marketplace. In-depth expertise can have great merit, especially in select disciplines, and can certainly be encouraged and supported. At the same time, workers gaining a broader range of knowledge in a variety of fields and across different disciplines will be able to apply this greater understanding to a multitude of functions and opportunities when such needs arise.

Mapping Skills and Competencies

The concept of rotating a majority of your organization's employees to engage them is not lightly proposed or contemplated. In a large organization, the logistics, potential complexity, and prospective challenges can be significant. HR technology is emerging and being refined to support and facilitate such plans—by mapping an employee's skills and capabilities, for example, as well as mapping the requirements of all relevant existing corporate roles.

Overlaying the two maps—one of individual competencies and the other of specific job requirements—both employer and employee can then review the closest adjacent positions that might be relevant,[107] and an appropriate progression can be developed. Selection of suitable jobs for the plan would consider factors such as the individual's interest in the next and possible subsequent roles, the knowledge and skill requirements for specific roles, the needs of the business, and the career plans of colleagues—those in the team and elsewhere in the company—that might involve the same adjacent positions.

Once the possible options have been mapped, discussed, narrowed down, and decided upon, timeframes can be discussed, incorporating the movement of other colleagues as well. Training and coaching is essential to facilitate transitions, which can be integrated into augmented learning and development programs. These are important attraction and retention tools in fulfilling career-development commitments and objectives. All along, progression of the move is monitored, and the performance of the employee is reviewed frequently, to ensure the proper support is provided.

Different people have different capacities and propensities for adjusting and settling into new jobs and fields, and mapping strategies can be adjusted and tailored to each specific person to take this into account. A dip in productivity is to be expected with a move, and it is important to allow for this when someone is ramping up in a new position. Role transitions can be assisted by an open dialog between managers and team members, working together to discuss and tackle challenges that might surface. A substantial shift in mindset, both of managers and of the organization, can be promoted to enable initial and ongoing productive discussion where necessary.

Creating a Mentoring Culture

In an unfamiliar landscape, where there are new rules, operating practices, and career pathways, employees are being asked to be more adaptable and to work across departmental boundaries. In such scenarios, mentoring relationships can be very effective for facilitating progress within your company in multiple ways. The pairings can be purposefully generated but informally tracked, or matched and monitored carefully as part of a formal mentoring program. However, in both scenarios, there are multiple beneficial potential outcomes for your business. With numerous mentoring pairs throughout your company, and cultural values expressed that support genuine and trusting relationships, a compelling mentoring culture can develop.

First, mentoring pairs can comprise employees matched across functions, divisions, and teams, allowing people in different fields and parts of your company to get to know each other as well as each other's skills and projects. In sharing information about work and situations, silos can be more easily broken down, changes accelerated, new ideas tested, and employees moved around. The latter is especially important with new, latticed careers, so that employees can have a better understanding of other opportunities in different areas of the business.

Second, pairs can be created specifically to bridge intergenerational gaps and create relationships that can help employees of every generation and type to bond across your organization, improving their understanding of each other through increased one-on-one communication. The cross-generational mentoring pairs can enable younger colleagues to share their knowledge, such as useful applications and new technology ideas as practical solutions in nonthreatening situations. These can support timely advancement of technology integration across and within your company. At the same time, with fresher eyes on company practices, newer recruits can be encouraged to review accepted routines and contemplate new approaches. Novel concepts can then be voiced and tested within open and accepting mentoring discussions. Such conversations can be fruitful in expanding and accelerating changes relating to culture and mindset.

Similarly, with the purposeful bidirectional nature of a mentoring pair's interactions, the older colleague can share their own expertise and knowledge of the company in a situation where there is a neutral platform for exchanges. Younger recruits are keen to make progress and get advice to help them develop their career plans in the new, more self-directed environment. Older colleagues who are paired up as mentors have the experience to provide advice as to how to navigate challenges and take advantage of opportunities. They can also discover and support the hopes and aspirations of their younger colleagues at your company. Without divulging confidences, mentoring relationships can also help surface employee issues and concerns and improve understanding of how to encourage engagement and improve retention.

Finally, mentoring can really help fill in the void until programs incorporating latticed, customized career-development strategies and frameworks are more defined, developed, and implemented. Many people who are new to your organization and are early in their careers will have little comprehension of what is ahead and how to make progress. To engage and retain these new recruits, it is critical that the corporation helps them understand that it cares about them personally—is trying to nurture their potential, listen to their needs, and develop their strengths. Identifying a mentor for a new hire may be one of the most important next steps your company can take to demonstrate that.

At the same time, the prevailing environment is new to Baby Boomers and Generation X-ers as well—not to mention that they also have legacy habits born of traditional routines and experiences that might be encouraged to be reframed for the new scenarios.

However, employees of these earlier generations do have more experience in terms of understanding developments over the course of their own careers. They can at least use first principles to give thoughtful direction and share their experiences as regards how to handle a particular task, how to deal with certain managers, or how to analyze a problem and develop a particular solution. So, while they will not have all the answers, they can help create a way forward and make progress, engaging both parties in the mentoring pair in the process.

Developing Personal Business Plans

Making progress to support creation of individual career plans for each employee is an initiative that most companies' human resources departments will need time to be prepared and equipped for. Large companies will be challenged to handle the numbers involved. At the same time, requesting greater involvement from employees, whether in mentoring pairs or otherwise, can itself be a tool for engagement and retention.

For example, a private equity firm, concerned about retention and specifically the possibility of losing younger team members, tasked every employee below partner level with creating their own personal business plan. This concept is adaptable for all new work environments as employment and careers are experienced in more entrepreneurial settings. For an independent worker, the focus is on the person as their own enterprise—identifying a personal unique selling proposition (USP), positioning themself competitively, providing services, and generating revenue streams.

In a corporate setting, the process and outcome become a combined career-development and engagement tool. All workers participate fully, thinking about their own strengths, how to apply them, and what they might be interested in doing at the company in the medium- and long-term with these skills and talents. Employees are also directed to take their employer's perspective into account (for which parameters may be given) in developing and proposing appropriate roles for themselves now and in the future, detailing reasons and possible milestones for their future advancement.

At the private equity firm, each employee was advised to step back, take a first principles approach, and initially consider purely personal elements in creating a personal business plan. They were encouraged to seek inputs from colleagues, friends, and family to discover answers to such questions as "What are my talents and skills? What are my core strengths within that range? What do I enjoy doing the most, and does that align with my strengths? How much do I want to focus on these aspects going forward? What skills and capabilities would I like to add or believe I need? How do I see myself as uniquely-positioned? How would I like to enhance this position over time, or how do I think I would like to evolve it?"

The next stage for each person was thinking through how these elements were aligned with the needs of the business—immediately and in the medium term: "How can I best position myself at the company, considering my skills and strengths? How can I create the most value for the business, leveraging my current, and desired future, capabilities? What role(s) might be a good or better fit for me at the company? What future roles could be beneficial for my professional development? What roles would I like to experience over the next two to three (or more) years? What skills do I need to add to be well-positioned for these roles?"

There was also a consideration by the company for employees' "what next?" concerns and thoughts about potential future career experiences *outside* the organization. Whatever the size of the company, there may not be the diversity of roles or the ability to rotate certain employees. However, friendly, networked, or affiliated (including investment-portfolio) companies might be recommended to specific people with a "long-term, long-tail" talent perspective— i.e., that this could create long-term future value and benefits for the company. If a person leaves with the connections, support, and blessing of their employer, they become part of the network of talent that is outside the organization but remains linked.

A supported departure generates positive relationships with the next company the person works for. It also encourages the possibility of that person's return to the original organization once they have gathered additional experience that is beneficial to both the individual and the initial employer. This tactic is especially useful for companies that are not able to provide a variety of experiences to benefit their employees' careers over time. Instead, they can hope to gain from an employee's leaving to attain different work experience and skills and then coming back. In these cases, incentive packages and strategies can be aligned to encourage the flow of people back to the company. An example could be freezing an employee's vesting options upon their departure, with a clause to restart the vesting if the person returns to the company within an identified period, say five years.

The response to the personal-business-plan-development exercise at the private equity firm was overwhelmingly positive. In having had their inputs solicited from the outset, employees were delighted and engaged actively in the process of developing their personalized plans. Their perspectives were also illuminating with regard to their sense of their own strengths and offered new viewpoints about the business and what positions they foresaw might be interesting to them in the future at the company.

Employees' contributions were also extremely helpful for identifying what their target roles might be—in the short-, medium-, and longer-term—and where and how they were looking for support, input, coaching, and skill development over time. After the ensuing discussions—exploring the options and viable possibilities—each person was even more committed to their customized and agreed-upon career plan. It was very explicitly recognized that this was a living document for each person and would be revisited regularly and updated as desired or necessary from both sides.

One additional dimension revealed was a traditional, almost exclusive, emphasis on "hard," quantitative skills as part of the management's analysis of employees' career plans and prospects. After dialog with the leadership, "soft" skills, such as leadership, empathy, and people skills, were included with more specific weighting, realizing the increasing importance of these aspects in today's professional environment—among colleagues as well as in external relationships.

In such an evolving workplace, stability is in short supply—the only constant is change itself. Fostering these conversations can also give employees some sense of stability. If they have a better comprehension of their own capabilities and how these can be applied to develop their potential, they start to become accountable for their own sense of security. They can begin to feel more comfortable, with their sense of identity coming from within themselves, while their income—as well as their community and opportunities—still comes from the company.

The personal-business-plan-development process works best when approached by all parties with a proactive mindset and a first-principles approach to create an impartial forum for discussion. It is best facilitated carefully, with adjustable levels of guidance for workers on how to develop their plans. With the benefit of training and leveraging the final outputs, employees are likely to engage in their work more independently, having been tasked with reviewing themself as though they were their own personal enterprise. They can have more confidence in pursuing the opportunities they participated in identifying and confirmed their suitability to handle. Thinking entrepreneurially also helps workers learn to track their own performance, develop their skills, find ways to innovate, and increase their effectiveness. This entrepreneurial approach is beneficial for the sake of innovation in a corporate setting, and these days such "intrapreneurial" attitudes are being encouraged at large firms.

The personal-business-plan exercise is also an effective way to gather understanding of employees' desires to have different experiences, try new roles, and gain new skills and talents within your company. Employees are thereby efficiently providing human resources with detailed data about their preferred individual career development that can then be explored, negotiated, and planned for. In addition, the involved management of all the different career plans also yields helpful information as to your future hiring needs, their roles and skills—for short- or long-term employment.

Interpreting Resumes

The evolution of careers has already had a profound impact on modern resumes, which can look very different from traditional ones. Corporate HR professionals or the managers involved in hiring might not yet be familiar with differences that are surfacing, especially with younger prospective hires. If the new working context has not been fully understood and accepted, the format and job-profile changes can evoke different responses and might result in good potential candidates being overlooked.

As some job tenures shorten, careers become more fragmented, and continuous full-time employment becomes less common, many more resumes are functionally-organized instead of following the previously standard **chronologically-formatted resume**. A **functionally-formatted resume** emphasizes skills and capabilities and highlights how they have been applied in relevant positions held or work accomplished. The intention of this layout is to focus on the talents of an individual, without stressing the length of the job or project work or any hiatus, which might distract or be misinterpreted by the reader. Varied work experience and skills are more easily presented in this manner, as are skills across disciplines and experience in different industry sectors.

This format contrasts with the more familiar, chronologically-formatted resume, which presents a compounding progression of jobs listed with sequential dates, titles, and types of tasks fulfilled, as well as work-related achievements in those roles. Such a resume is well-designed to emphasize the accomplishments of a person who has worked continuously, likely in one discipline and one industry sector, incrementally moving up the associated corporate ladder for their entire career.

Nowadays, there is much less uniformity about a typical "career identity" that recruiters may have been accustomed to looking for when trying to fill a particular position. Going forward, an individual is much less likely to be associated with only one discipline or sector—such as being a "marketing person" or a "retail person." Instead, someone is most likely to have a series of different careers, changing how and where they apply particular skills and focus on different interests and strengths. For example, someone with a retail background might apply their skills at a company with an online store, and then later work for an organization that provides services with which customers engage on their phones, in a commerce-like transactional manner. At the same time, employers are increasingly leveraging new and diverse skills and talents. So, they will also be looking for different elements in someone's resume to ascertain a good fit for the less-defined and adaptable roles they are hiring for.

When reviewing resumes these days, recruiters, executives, and managers can usefully consider a thoughtful approach or reaction to shorter tenures than they have typically been used to seeing. Project and part-time work experience is best discussed before any particular interpretation is warranted. It is advisable to weigh the full combination of someone's hard and soft skills, specific expertise, experience, and intention (to apply effort). An open mindset and adaptability to work form and function are also important to evaluate, depending on the role and needs. A similar range of elements is also relevant when reviewing the backgrounds and assessing the expertise and fit of long-term consultants and even project hires with your company and the work to be done. Certain people work better liaising with teams, while others work most effectively when they are completely independent.

At the same time, how independent contractors choose to market themselves or connect with companies such as yours may differ greatly. One person might prefer to outsource their sales to an umbrella organization that liaises with your company when specific skills are needed. Another might prefer to develop direct relationships by doing their own networking. Different people can certainly choose a range of options to see what works best for their particular service propositions and how their offering resonates with the companies they prefer to work with. It is worthwhile to explore and understand different alternative sources and what combination might be most appropriate for your organization. As mentioned in chapter 9, the hiring process for—and ongoing oversight of—independent workers may be modified to be coordinated by human resources instead of procurement as their in-person and virtual presence at your company increases.

As workers of all generations face the different elements of transitioning to the Future-of-Work environment, increased and focused learning and development programs can assist them in understanding how to navigate the changes. Then they can optimize their personal adaptation relating to their work profiles and career development, enhancing their engagement and performance. Training and coaching initiatives are witnessing new interest and activity. Executives, managers, and employees are now proactively requesting coaching and classes, in contrast to some typical attitudes that training is only for compliance purposes. The head of career development at one leading New York hospital group noted that seminars on leadership in a changing environment are now in great demand. Since the transformation we are undergoing is very much in progress and will be through 2030 at least, augmented ongoing learning and development is recommended to support your company in transition.

At the same time, the pace of business is not going to slow down any time soon. Employees are also looking for education and support to help them keep on top of technology changes and up-to-date about marketplace developments. The younger cadres are most engaged by short, entertaining video content, while others may prefer audio, graphics, or text. In-person and online content, seminars, and classes can be developed and provided internally or through an increasing number of outsourced providers. As new personalized career paths incorporate rotation to other disciplines and divisions at a company, internal training and external courses allow employees to develop the new skills or achieve a certification they need. These activities both enhance general capabilities at your company and provide a powerful retention tool for employees who understand their employer's commitment to their careers and ongoing development.

In a competitive and rapidly-changing marketplace, the development of your workforce—both employees and independent contractors—becomes a critical and strategic lever. Maximizing their engagement through personalization can be achieved by means of a compelling combination of ongoing elements and choices, including career development, mentoring, and internally- and externally-delivered training and courses.

Chapter 11 Takeaways

- **First Principles**: Consider the profound and far-reaching implications of the demise of the "permanent" full-time job and the linear, continuous career path that is shifting to a more latticed model. Reflect on your company's employees' overall career experiences and how they can be managed optimally going forward. Think about how individual careers can best be planned, with employees' involvement and contributions to share the workload and improve the outcomes. Contemplate having more experienced employees helping newer recruits navigate your organization.

- **Priorities**:
  - Engagement—Especially as careers evolve and are becoming more self-directed, career development is a significant area for activating and engaging employees. Involving them in the process also motivates them to own the outcomes and to

participate proactively in the planning and ongoing evolution of their careers.

□ Personalization—Careers are becoming customized to the individual, with latticed pathways that are unique to each person. This major shift involves the strategic participation of human resources, coaching support, and new HR technology to help map, plan, and monitor.

□ Integration—With every employee's career taking a different pathway, possibly across departments and even divisions, greater communication, merging, and cross-pollination of internal talent pools increases in importance.

□ Choice—New career definitions and options—including lateral and diagonal career moves—are changing career development and planning. Employees can be incentivized by the possibilities of growing and expanding their experiences in a new variety of ways.

- **Evaluation:**

  □ What percentage of your company's employees does your human resources department currently actively engage with for career development and planning purposes?

  □ What options are employees offered relating to career-progression possibilities—including lateral and diagonal moves?

  □ How are employees' skills mapped against company positions to determine fit for subsequent roles?

- How are those employees supported with learning and development initiatives to augment their skills and move into new roles?

- How many people in the organization are involved in formal and informal mentoring relationships that help employees navigate the company and individual careers?

- How well does your company culture support mentoring relationships?

- **Metrics**: Examples include: Increase in number of employees who have personalized, latticed career plans; increase in employees' satisfaction with your company's career-planning process and initiatives; number of employee mentoring pairs that work on career-development issues, and increase in that number over time; increase in coaching hours provided to employees to support career-development planning; and increase in number of employees whose competencies have been mapped against company roles.

CHAPTER 12

THE ORGANIZATION AS
A LIVING ORGANISM

Chose a job you love, and you will never have to work a day in your life.
CONFUCIUS

S am Suess looks forward to his workweek. On Mondays, he
is usually working from home, as he does on Thursdays, so,
by not commuting, he saves time and money and reduces
his stress and carbon footprint. On Tuesdays and Wednesdays, he
drives forty minutes to the main corporate office and works there
from 10 o'clock a.m. to 6 o'clock p.m. for coordinated internal and
external meetings, and on Fridays he usually walks the fifteen minutes
to the local co-working office base, where he works 11 o'clock a.m. to
7 o'clock p.m., for his weekly coordination or brainstorming sessions
with one or more of the developers who prefer later hours.

Suess also has good interactions with his colleagues in the office, using video applications such as Skype and Google+, depending on whom he is speaking with and where he is at the time. He is in tune with his coworkers' timing and location needs, and they accommodate his. He shares his projects and updates openly with relevant team members via cloud-based project-management tools. Suess talks to his boss regularly, and especially frequently when starting a project, until all the details, dates, and milestones have been clearly defined and agreed upon.

Suess manages four teams of people at the moment. One team is made up of freelancers and is entirely virtual. The freelancers were hired as an outsourced group and typically work together on projects. Another team consists of full-time employees who work remotely or at one of the corporate offices, depending on the day. If they feel they need to work together in person on something—perhaps a kick-off meeting with a new team, a mid-project brainstorming session, or a challenging problem that crops up—they usually coordinate where to meet two weeks ahead of time. The other two teams are composed of both employees and independent contractors who work regularly with the company and that division. In fact, one of the contractors was actually an employee a few years before but now only works on select, smaller projects.

Suess uses a variety of web-based tools to interact and communicate with different team members individually or with groups together. He also shares information broadly within the company about the progress of projects, so that other loosely-defined divisions are kept up to speed, as they might be affected by revisions, issues, or developments.

Suess checks in with his supervisor every week, to talk about his progress and discuss any team-member issues and revisions to milestones, before confirming his goals. He reevaluates his role and the types of projects he works on with his boss every quarter. If there is another position or project he would rather be involved with one or more years ahead, they discuss how he can best attain the skills he will need to transition to the desired role, over what time period. Last year, Suess actually took a part-time, four-week course that built up his capabilities in some cutting-edge robotics applications that allowed him to adapt a few of their products for a new target market. It was exciting work, and he hopes to become more involved with the artificial-intelligence division's work after another part-time course he will do in a few months' time.

Suess loves to run marathons and organizes to be off work certain Fridays to allow him time to travel and acclimate before his races, applying his monthly fitness benefit toward travel costs. His company has an unlimited vacation policy, and he has taken between eighteen and twenty-one days a year, depending on his project load, market activity, family, and work-team needs. He hasn't missed one of his planned vacations since he rejoined this company full time four years ago after two years elsewhere gaining other valuable expertise. Sam enjoys what he does. The variety of environments, projects, and people keep him interested, and he is able to be dedicated to his passion for running, as well.

It seems that Suess is in a role where he is "working human." This is a compelling new phrase that qualifies a company's approach to the employee experience. It sounds very different from what most people have been dealing with in their work environments. And it is.

If we recognize our world as the ecosystem it is, and the business marketplace as an integral part of that—rather than a separate, mechanical, and inhumane realm—then we can also acknowledge the reality of ourselves as human workers within that environment.

We may then reframe our approach to get the most out of our labor force in a way that is reciprocal and self-supporting.

At the beginning of the Industrial Era, when we were still struggling to survive and understand how best to utilize and improve the efficiency of the machines we had created, we prioritized machines over human labor. Thankfully, we have progressed in many ways since then. We have developed much more sophisticated machines and a much more informed understanding of our human workforce—including what kind of treatment does and does not actually stimulate workers to perform at their best for their employer.

We can now realize the rewards of this progress and apply our advanced technology and comprehension in designing company ecosystems that accept and respond to the natural reality of the core workforce. If we optimize for this, then organizations will be able to reflect and evolve for—and with—the living organisms that are their lifeblood. In so doing, we will be best-positioned to be most productive and to leverage our most human, creative strengths.

Being Human

I would be so bold as to suggest that we are not actually very good at "being human." Not in the workplace, anyway. Not yet. In our efforts to reap the substantial benefits of machine efficiency from the start of the Industrial Age, we focused on our machines and tailored our work and environment to suit them, not us. We created machine-worthy fixed, monolithic structures to house them and then had to work there ourselves as well—in environments that were almost antithetical to human nature. Workers' roles were to facilitate maximum machine utility and output. For the most part, we have not paid much attention to the potential consequences of this.

Increased output and higher gross domestic product (GDP) were the emphases, in line with the government's great concern about having enough food to feed the fast-growing population.

However, as noted earlier, we have seen productivity levels stall and then decline, and engagement is very low and steady. We now know that human workers make errors, especially when they are not interested or get bored. Motivation is not just about being paid so that there is food on the table. We have noticed that society's current dynamics and labor composition have put a great strain on workers, since they have not been able to adapt the traditional working profiles—even though the rest of their lives and their economic needs have changed.

In parallel, as we connect the billions of machines that we have created in order that they communicate and serve our needs more quickly and effectively, our machines are now both much more powerful *and* user-friendly. They are touch-, motion-, and voice-controlled and activated, responding in ways that are much more human and more intuitive to use. We are making robots that look and sound more human, giving humans robotics-enhanced prosthetics, embedding chips in humans to supplement damaged nerves, and more. Where are the lines of separation as they become part of us or we become humanoids, at the same time as "real" and "virtual" become out-of-date delineations?

We are now leveraging machines more as tools that enhance our capabilities or that do the tasks we do not want to do. However, as machines have proliferated, we desire—perhaps even need—to reassert our control and confirm just who is serving whom. Automation and robots are already challenging humans' competitive competence and redefining our existing roles. There are virtual assistants such as "Amy" from x.ai that (or who?) may be mistaken for human—as I once did![108] We have even started to contemplate the idea that falling in love with a computer program is possible—as in the film *Her*, in which a lonely writer (played by Joaquin Phoenix) falls in love with his computer's new operating system.

Furthermore, in tandem, business as a whole is moving away from the impersonal and one-sided to the personalized and connected. Customers want to know more about the companies they are buying from and those companies' values, to find out if they are aligned. For example, Apple raised the ire of customers over the possibility that it implicitly supported worker abuse: Were its products being built in factories where there might be child laborers or where workers were being mistreated? Customers want to know more about the people who make the products they buy or deliver the services they need. They care about being aligned with a company's values and sometimes the employees as well. They might even want to be part of the same community. If the corporate values are jarring or discordant they may go elsewhere. Customers are also engaging more deeply in the actual product cycle and refinements, responding to surveys to make specific comments and recommendations.

So, it is high time we understand and celebrate the best of who we are as human beings, engage everyone fully, and optimize and personalize the workplace accordingly. It may well not be cleanly or clearly defined. Human beings are, by nature, messy. We are each unique. We are capable of brilliance and error. These characteristics are what we want, and need, to capture and allow for—mistakes, and unintended consequences, have led to some of the most important developments of the modern era, such as penicillin, X-rays, and the pacemaker.

Organizations focused on adapting to the very human qualities and characteristics of their workers will be able to promote much healthier—and create much more productive—personalized working environments. As you take the next steps to create the Future-of-Work environment at your company, your employees and other workers will be happier and more engaged, do better work, come up with better ideas, be more loyal, and stay longer. This is what progress looks like.

"I need someone in Superhuman Resources."

You are making an important choice to take the next, sometimes challenging, steps to adapt. As a reminder, much data is referenced throughout the book and in the endnotes to support the various recommendations and assertions I have made, and there is much more behind that if you need further convincing in a particular area, or need help persuading anyone in your organization.

Evolve or Die

A little melodrama is possibly in order here. I am far from the only one who is convinced that some, possibly many, long-established organizations will disappear if, or rather when, they do not transition to new ways of working. Companies that are "sick"—that do not realize how evolving circumstances are impacting them and do not take steps to find out what they need to do to improve their health—may well not adapt quickly enough. A portion of them will simply not survive. I have already noted the accelerated turnover of the S&P 500 in recent decades. Now there is significantly more in flux—with not only external marketplace changes but also the numerous ongoing internal workplace and workforce changes that have been discussed. The complexity of addressing it all successfully can be substantial.

Evolution is about survival of the fittest. That doesn't mean the strongest or the fastest but rather the ones who are best able to adapt and flourish in the prevailing conditions, even if circumstances keep changing. Fixed structures and linear, repetitive, machine-bound tasks do not promote human productivity—but rather the natural flow of relationships and the sharing of information freely within an organization catalyzes creative discourse and effective response.

There are a variety of reasons why certain organizations will flounder and collapse. It might be because they are not able to attract any good new hires and have lost too many of their employees. This could occur if they do not update working formats and tasks are not modified to match the needs of the business with worker skills and to develop the potential of the workforce, as Big Ass Solutions does (in chapter 5). It might be that they are not tracking customer reactions and changing demands, so their products or services are not updated quickly enough to respond to market demands, and their sales fall off dramatically.

It might be that they haven't bothered to articulate their core values in ways that resonate with their current employees and con-tractors, as the 86 Company has done in its company manifesto. It might be that they haven't sought to reduce the layers of hierarchy to enable the multidirectional exchanges of information that the business needs, as at Sakara, where they are keen that the voices of all employees are heard and ideas incorporated. It might be that the static cubicles and cordoned-off office layout is not recognizing the different activities of workers, such that they cannot collaborate effectively to develop the next innovative iterations of products or services. It could be a multiplicity of these reasons and many others that are encompassed by the Future-of-Work changes.

A symbiotic relationship between humans and nature best explains our survival amid the extinction of other species. It has been our ability to adapt to change—to organize, to collaborate, to adjust to our surroundings, to learn, and to create—that drove our advancements and continues to lead our progress to this day. Without developing and sharing tools, resources, and capabilities with one another and adapting to our environment quickly and adeptly, we would have perished rather quickly in harsh environments. In the same way, it is important to recognize that your company is the sum of many moving parts. It takes real effort to understand, integrate, and support your workforce in order for their individual—and your company's—full potential to be realized.

Evolution is a constant, although the pace of it may change. In acknowledging this, the objective is to be focused on looking forward and not backward. Leadership throughout your company can embrace the evolutionary needs and incorporate them appropriately in a phased approach, wherever and however makes sense for your organization. Choices abound, and trial and error is a suitable process for incremental and steady forward progress. It's all about taking small steps to reach where you want to go, no matter how far that may be. As you advance, always lead with your cultural tenets first, with a focus on your talent's needs.

People are at the core of the Future-of-Work changes. The more your company "feels" like an ecosystem, the easier it will be to "humanize" the culture, purpose, policies, and overall working environment. Furthermore, the more satisfied, personally-empowered, and individually-engaged your workers are, the more your company will feel like a living organism, reflecting the sum total of all the individuals working under its overall umbrella. As its structure becomes a framework, it will be able to adjust to the marketplace, seasonal needs, and the economic climate, as well as its own growth and fluctuating body of workers, expanding and contracting naturally. Employees and contractors will ebb and flow depending on the rhythm of work and personal needs and locations, as well as different projects launching and being completed.

Nor does your company, as an entity, live in a vacuum. Every business is an ecosystem, which is also part of a larger environment that extends much further. The edges of your organization will become less distinct as employees come and go, collaborative business projects stretch beyond company-based teams, and other firms become interconnected with yours. Learning how to coexist successfully within an interconnected and increasingly-integrated and vibrant ecosystem is also important for your company's overall survival and success. Your organization's capacity to thrive will be based on a combination of its role, competitive positioning, and thoughtful participation in the overall marketplace. In addition, it will involve your proactive and informed intention to engage and personalize the experience of your very human talent, each of whom is a critical member of an adaptable and responsive integrated living and evolving business community.

Chapter 12 Takeaways

- **First Principles:** Consider how your company can optimize for the most "human" talents of your workforce and promote their well-being. Contemplate how each person's individual nature can best be acknowledged and their human skills and strengths nurtured and employed. Think about the planning of your next steps to ensure that your company is evolving in a timely manner. Develop fundamental approaches that emphasize flexibility so that your company can continue to respond and adapt appropriately as surrounding circumstances evolve.

- **Priorities:**

  - Engagement—Treating all your workers as "humans" is the best way to engage them and help them perform optimally. Customer engagement is also important, and the human stories from your company's workers can be valuable for creating those connections.

  - Personalization—New technologies are more intuitive, with more human-friendly interfaces, which can be used for improved effect with your workers. Human beings are "messy," which is important to recognize and accommodate in planning for and transitioning to your company's Future-of-Work environment.

  - Integration—Incorporating advanced technology can facilitate better interactions and communications between dispersed workers, supporting your corporate community. With an emphasis on talent and employee well-being, seamless integration of aligned policies and operating practices can have a profound and positive impact on performance and productivity.

- □ Choice—Humans respond positively to having options and more control over their work and lives than in "traditional" work environments. Increasing autonomy and alternatives offered to workers will improve overall well-being with specific benefits of greater creativity, productivity, and lower turnover.

- **Evaluation**:
  - □ What choices are you offering to your workers to allow them to adjust their working profile to accommodate their overall corporate *and* noncorporate activities, understanding their human conditions?

  - □ To what extent does management appreciate and leverage the human creativity of each of your workers?

  - □ How are you enabling your workers to express their human creativity?

  - □ How are you expressing the culture of your company in terms of human values that your workers can relate to emotionally and even spiritually?

  - □ What emphasis does your company have on increasing the well-being of each of your employees?

- **Metrics:** The impact of "working-human" initiatives can be felt across the organization, as well as through the greater ecosystem. Examples include: increase in productivity, reduction of turnover, increase in sales (customers' perception of how employees are treated), increase in engagement, increase in employee satisfaction, increase in customer satisfaction, improvement in overall employee health, and reduction in employee stress levels.

CHAPTER 13

YOUR PLAN FOR PROGRESS

Without deviation from the norm, progress is not possible.
FRANK ZAPPA

"The norm's" time is over—relating to work, at least. Traditional management practices that do not emphasize employees are being replaced. For a business to be able to project strong growth and success going forward, its workers will need to be successful first. They will need to feel good about the work they do, or they will stop showing up—physically or mentally. As we know from chapter 1, the majority of employees already have.

What makes employees feel good in today's tumultuous world of employment? The future workplace is looking radically different from most of today's traditional work cultures and management structures. Some forward-thinking leaders are making strides in finding out what will resonate with their employees, from Tony Hsieh at Zappos working on implementing Holacracy's radical flat self-management model and Carey Smith's consensus approach to decision-making at Big Ass Solutions, to Dan Price at Gravity Payments deciding to pay every employee at least $70,000 and Gavin McGarry at Jumpwire Media having new hires propose their salaries. These are just a few of the competitive talent strategies that employers are exploring to get out in front of the employment changes that employees are looking for in order to engage them.

The most daring strategies are getting more reactions—good and bad—than employers could have possibly anticipated. Should we be surprised? No—transformation IS disruptive. Reactions are born of excitement about the possibilities as well as fear about how to cope with the changes forecast. The good, the bad, and the ugly about all this is that we are *all* in it together! For all but a few, this is mostly unfamiliar territory. Some changes may be small, others larger—but in combination, the total effect is significant. However, even if someone has been wanting a flexible, engaging, personalized, and happier work environment and embraces the changes in theory, in *practice*, it may be another matter altogether. Habits are known and "safe," even if they are actually somewhat uncomfortable.

Yes, there is *much* adaptation ahead, wherever you are starting from, however much progress you have made so far. So, what is to be accomplished and how can you get it done? What are the next steps to implement changes in the least disruptive way to your organization and workers? What's the plan?!

Your Framework for Progress

I have shared much research and understanding about what is in process, what is anticipated ahead, why we are here, and why it is clear that there is no turning back. I am also extremely aware that the amount of information I have shared—which I have gathered, journeyed through, assimilated, and analyzed over several years— can be overwhelming. My intention is that it all be both interesting and useful, to inform and support your next steps towards a much more positive working environment for your company. This way you can start—or continue—to advance to circumstances where your employees are more engaged and productive and your business is more adaptable and responsive and able to succeed within the new working and market circumstances.

A reasonable plan to deal properly with everything that I have thrown at you is a multilayered and involved process that cannot be described quickly. However, after giving you so much information, I would like to ensure you have at least the outline of one approach or methodology mapped out that you can work through and apply.

To create a plan for the next (and possibly first concrete) steps of the transition for your organization, I recommend that a thoughtful composite concept be envisioned for your company for its Future-of-Work environment. The idea is to create a relatively thorough projection or future sketch, as noted in chapter 1, of the progress that is the desired goal for your organization. This forecast may then be explained in its component parts, understood, and advanced towards as the overall and detailed objectives of the plan. To accomplish this, I recommend you assemble a core transition team from across your company to help you—selecting members of different divisions, functions, management levels, age, experience, and background, and ensuring a broad diversity of perspective.

An important inherent assumption here is that you have already achieved the buy-in of the key stakeholders at your company. I realize this is far from a given and requires data, discussion, and debate. See the endnotes for a list of persuasive data and useful references that can help support the next steps toward your Future-of-Work ecosystem.

Since the working circumstances will continue to be dynamic for the foreseeable future, I propose that a framework concept be used to develop your future sketch and plan, as it is notionally both multidimensional and flexible. The form of the framework is created by the Pillars, which I identified at the beginning of the book. These are the theoretical "columns" that support your organization and which I have taken you through as you have advanced through the book. To recap, I have grouped them as: Technology; Culture and Mindset; Leadership, Transparency, and Hierarchy; Productivity, Performance, and Creativity; Policies, Frameworks, and Environment; and Careers, Freelancers, and Learning.

As explained earlier, these Pillars embody the key areas that are evolving in the transformation to new ways of working. Together, your transition team may amend the groupings to be most appropriate for your company, depending on the organizational scheme that makes sense for your workforce and business going forward. The Pillars are flexible and revisable in composition and relative to each other. However, they are critical in concept, as the stakes that currently hold up the "platform" of your company, and up which the platform will rise as you make progress in each of these areas and across them all.

Projecting Your Pillars

In order to project your company's optimal overall Future-of-Work environment, the first step of the process is to forecast a subset of future scenarios, one for each of the Pillars, which can then be rolled up thoughtfully into a coherent vision of and for the future. During tumultuous times, when much change is anticipated, I recommend that your transition team adopt a first-principles approach, as I noted at the beginning of the book. The goal is for you and all the team members to step back from current operating strategies and practices and evaluate the fundamental components of each area of your business afresh. Information from this book, together with data from many referenced and additional research studies, can be used to understand prevailing and predicted changing marketplace conditions. These will encompass your company as well as your competition and the progress plans they embark upon. The transition team can be tasked with asking basic questions about your business and company in order to develop the outline of a "future-proofed" environment.

The questions include high-level concepts comprising the more fundamental aspects as well as those that are more company-specific but still taking an arm's-length approach. Examples include:

- How can we create the best working environment to attract and retain the best talent going forward?

- What are the essential elements that will engage employees to perform at their best?

- What kind of physical environments will stimulate employees' creativity and enhance their concentration to improve their productivity?

- What kind of office presence does the company really need—and why, for whom, for what, and where?

In particular areas, more specific questions can include:

- What are the core values that we believe capture the essence of our company culture and that will attract relevant new talent?

- What specific career-planning processes are going to allow our employees to develop their potential and engage them through their own involvement?

- How can we increase customer-response time by creating cross-functional teams as well as deliberately encouraging employees to connect across divisions?

- What technical connectivity, applications, devices, and platforms are going to support our workers fully, both those working in the office and employees and nonemployees working remotely?

Inputs and suggestions can be solicited and gathered from clients and customers, vendors, and contractors, together with survey responses from employees. I advise including all the players in your company's ecosystem—all these constituents will be part of your future and will be contributors in accomplishing any plan. It is therefore beneficial to collect inputs from widespread sources, and involving and engaging participants in the process can help get their buy-in. These parties' efforts will certainly be needed or helpful when executing your plan. Many people in and around your firm may also already have some great ideas about non-incremental changes as well as innovative adjustments.

After data gathering and thorough review and analysis, your team can then formulate a range of hypothetical scenarios for each of the Pillars in order to compose sketch descriptions of possible relevant desired future environments. It is important to incorporate the Priorities of engagement, personalization, integration, and choice carefully into the area-specific goals and modifications during this process. Projected elements may be similar, slightly reworked, or very different from your company's current operating configuration. The different possibilities can then be narrowed down, and then, as the concept for each Pillar is formed and selected, the pervasive core tenets, such as cultural aspects, can be harmonized throughout the Pillars and framework. Then, in combination, the future sketches of the Pillars create a composite vision and framework that supports your future company platform, elevated by updated, advanced elements in each area.

This projection of your working environment is not definitive, nor can it be. It will be influenced by external circumstances and determined by the nuanced interpretations of your workforce as they implement plans to achieve it. Instead, it will evolve as the environment does and will be edited and updated to stay current and continue to motivate everyone at your company. Now you have to work out where you are, so that you can start the journey to get where you want to go.

Evaluating Your Company's Status

The next step in the process of building your plan for progress is to assess your company's current status with regard to Future-of-Work advancement thus far. It is important to do this *after* working out where you want to get to, or it will be even harder to detach from current conditions and operating practices. The aim is to recognize where you are relative to each of the areas as discussed in previous chapters. There are no "marks" or objective delineations. However, it is essential to create a baseline and understand the originating point from which your company will be starting or moving (further) on from.

This allows your transition team to have benchmarks to monitor progress for each of the Pillars. Milestones and metrics for tracking are critical for demonstrating achievement and advances against plan objectives as well as showing the positive impact of Future-of-Work changes, permitting ongoing commitment and investment of time, effort, energy, and, where needed, funds. Thus, measurement enables your company to register where meaningful advances are being made and where further encouragement or effort is needed to make headway.

In addition to relevant questions included in earlier chapters' takeaways, the following are sample questions to help your transition team gather the data to evaluate your company's current status in the transition to a suitable Future-of-Work environment:

Technology

- To what extent is your company leveraging technology within core operations?

- Have your IT professionals suggested any new integrated applications that could dramatically change the way the company does business?

- How was any such proposal received?

- Does your company have any new competitors in your sector or niche that operate very differently from your business by leveraging technology in very different ways than your organization?

- Has your company's executive team carefully considered the pros and cons of how technology is best used to optimize how the business is run, including delivering what your customers really want?

- Do you use cloud-based project-management tools?

- How are remote and in-office workers being supported in terms of applications for communication and collaboration?

- How up-to-date are the applications and other tools that your employees are using?

- How are freelancers and consultants being enabled to work seamlessly, and securely, with and around your employees?

- Do you support a variety of devices to enable multi-platform creativity?

Culture and Mindset

- Where is your company in terms of understanding and articulating its culture *in writing*?

- To what extent have specific corporate values and purpose been identified and incorporated into corporate-culture–related documents?

- Are the same ideas already communicated clearly in hiring messaging, on-boarding documents, and customer and employee communications and activities?

- How often are the cultural values discussed, reflected in executive behavior, recognized, and supported?

- What is the corporate mindset that is recognized and aligns with the culture?

- Do executives and employees alike recognize and promote the corporate mindset as being one that will advance the company's success going forward?

Leadership, Transparency, and Hierarchy

- How empathetic are your company's leaders—from CEO to senior executives and managers?

- How are decisions typically made—only at the top, or are employee inputs frequently incorporated and do they influence final decisions?

- Is your company's leadership team already considering or experimenting with new alternatives to engage all your employees, not just the highest performers?

- How forward-thinking are any new ways of working that are currently being contemplated for implementation?

- Are leadership's communications internally- and externally-consistent? Are they coherent with your company culture?

- How strong is the identity of the company?

- How well-aligned with the corporate identity is leadership throughout the company?

- How open is leadership with employees about good *and bad* company news?

- How much information is shared with all employees, not just the senior ones?

- How much do you include your extended talent pool in corporate communications?

- Who writes and who approves all your internal corporate communications?

- How does your company respond to negative customer feedback?

- How quickly does your company respond to customer feedback?

- How often are employees' opinions solicited, and on what range of topics?

- How much is employee feedback recognized and incorporated into relevant business operations?

- How many layers of management are there in your organization?

- Has this number decreased over the last decade?

- What is the average age of executive leadership?

- How much are younger employees involved in the company's strategic decisions and leadership, especially relating to technology-based initiatives?

Productivity, Performance, and Creativity

- How actively are individuals and groups supported in different environments to stimulate creativity?

- How is risk tolerated in your company, and how is failure responded to?

- How are insights from successes and failures captured and incorporated into future projects?

- How inclusive are the hiring policies of your company?

- Are your employees comfortable with the current diversity of your company's leadership and workforce?

- How quickly is your market evolving, and what kind of customer-feedback loop and responsiveness are you currently faced with and anticipating in the future?

- What would be the optimal processes to achieve the kind of response time that you estimate would give you a competitive advantage?

- To what degree do you feel innovation has been enabled through collaboration-physically and virtually?

- How would different teams best accomplish the necessary tasks—in terms of interacting, brainstorming together, working across departments, and communicating?

Policies, Framework, and Environment

- Are your policies consistent with your corporate culture and values?

- Do you know which policies your employees really care about?

- Have you adapted any policies as a result of employee feedback?

- How effectively are key policies implemented?

- Do senior executives advocate for new policies and set the example for new behavior for all employees that is consistent with corporate culture and messaging?

- Does your company's organizational structure allow the versatility to pivot quickly, if necessary, when making decisions or adapting to market changes?

- Is your office environment coherent with your culture?

- How do you enable and support individual and group work—both physically and virtually?

- How much does HR collaborate with IT and facilities management to support all your workers' needs?

- How could the dismantling of any boundaries between silos in your company augment the speed of interactions and improvements?

Careers, Freelancers, and Learning

- How many hours of training does each of your employees ask for, and how many do they get, per year?

- Do you know what each of your employees wants to do over the next three years?

- Do they have the ability to choose a course to enroll in each year to develop themselves professionally?

- Do you provide a variety of training modules that employees can take to augment their skills to benefit the company and their career development?

- Are you getting employees involved in identifying their career aspirations and interests?

- Are you still in contact with former employees, and prospective hires who did not convert, as an extended talent pool?

- How much are you leveraging part-time employees, project freelancers, and longer-term consultants?

- Have you developed a strategy for your external talent?

- How do you ensure independent contractors are a good fit culturally if you plan to engage them more than once over the long term?

- Do you have any employees who have become consultants and vice versa as the needs of the business change?

- How are you supporting your nonemployees technically and otherwise, so they can collaborate effectively with your employees?

Personalization, Engagement, Integration, and Choice

- How much has your company adapted work situations for each employee?

- Has workplace flexibility been implemented formally or informally at your company?

- Is it offered to all personnel or only some people?

- Are all options offered or only a few?

- What percentage of employees uses flexible work arrangements?

- Do you help your employees identify their strengths and create a personalized working profile?

- Have you surveyed your employees to find out how engaged they are?

- How often do you monitor their engagement and satisfaction?

- Has your company tried to find out what would help employees be more productive?

- Do your benefits match what your employees actually want?

- Does your CIO or technology lead work closely with the other business leads to support their operations and integrate relevant new applications appropriately?

- Are technology and "big data" viewed as tools or drivers for your business units?

- How timely is the data that is being used to make decisions in different areas of your company?

- Do you have strong business strategists within your technology team?

- How integrated are your disciplines—human resources, information technology, and facilities management in particular?

The Future of Work is focused on talent, so it is important to find out what workers actually want, not what the transition team or anyone else thinks they want. Real needs and desires can be very different from the needs that the team might expect, or fear, that employees will have. Surveying your employees, and even some of your consultants, is key to working out the parameters for your specific situation, business, and unique set of workers.

Once responses to these questions and many more like them are collated and reviewed for each Pillar and Priority, a description for the current status of every area can be crafted with themes taken into account. Compiling these, a starting framework can be outlined. Detail for this baseline sketch will be important, both in defining the metrics that will be used to measure and guide your company's progress relative to each Pillar and Priority and in creating the plan for advancing towards your projected Future-of-Work environment.

Developing Your Plan for Progress

After completing the future sketch and starting framework in reasonable detail, your transition team will have information with which to formulate your company's plan for progress. For each Pillar, the next step in this process is to plot the starting framework's "coordinates" and map them to those of the future sketch that you are trying to achieve. Connection of the data-point pairs will give both direction and prospective "destinations" for each Pillar, while acknowledging that the "end points" will be revised over time as circumstances continue to evolve.

While many variables are involved and changes anticipated, your company's plan can then be developed using the initial, directional, and anticipated-destination information for each Pillar. You can then review and analyze carefully what and how elements are to change for each area within each Pillar grouping in order to advance. These changes also incorporate important adaptations relating to the four Priorities that are essential to emphasize in a compelling and progressive working environment. With an understanding of the alterations required to bridge the difference between the data points, your company's transition team can then formulate strategies and tactics to govern the way forward. They can work closely with relevant members of specific departments and divisions depending on the Pillar area or Priority theme in question.

How adaptation of any particular element is planned for at your organization will depend on the existing status of each and every area and Pillar and their component elements, as they are all interrelated and interdependent. Other aspects impacting the plan are also unique to your company's current situation and operations—such as the products and services your business produces or provides; the type of different jobs the workers each do; how, when, and where they are working; and what engages each of them. In addition, how all companies around yours—whether customers, competitors, partners, or vendors—will transition to the Future-of-Work environment matters, too. Their changes will impact and influence your progress in the short-, medium-, and longer-term.

It will therefore be a reasonably-complicated plan, which is why it is helpful to break it down into manageable and identifiable components such as Pillars and Priorities, which may be addressed and trialed separately or in combination, in parallel or in sequence. In order to deconstruct some of the complexity, carefully arranging the order of the plan's rollout is essential, ensuring thoughtful selection and prioritization of areas to be addressed. There may be specific valid reasons, peculiar to your organization, that merit focusing on one aspect and trialing it with one discipline or office or division before another. However, Culture and Mindset is recommended to be on the critical path as the first Pillar to address for every organization, as it sits at the core and drives behaviors and actions throughout. Then other Pillars, areas, and elements may be sorted and ranked using clear parameters to identify which areas, and then particular elements, are the most appropriate or necessary for the initial or next pilot and then the rollout.

Trials are a beneficial means of introducing new Future-of-Work concepts over a chosen time period, as well as allowing incremental transition. Furthermore, the employees participating in the pilot can be engaged in the process, soliciting their inputs and suggestions for improvements and modifications before particular changes are rolled out further across the company. This is helpful for getting buy-in from employees in other areas ahead of executing new phases of the transition plan—step by step, area by area, element by element. As long as employees are aware of the efforts being made to make adjustments to improve their situation, listen to their comments and needs, and adapt to their situations, they can be forgiving of reasonable time delays, if those are necessary to ensure proper implementation.

A critical success factor is certainly to have coaching and training throughout the transformation period, with an emphasis on any areas that your transition or executive team believes might need extra support. Change-management support is extremely effective, and indeed has been proven critical, to adjust to and really benefit from new physical office environments. Add to that significant operational change, new flexible models, and work expectations, and training becomes mandatory for making successful adaptions.

Since we are in the midst of transformational times, it is essential to consider and incorporate the evolutionary aspect. Each Pillar and area will adapt and evolve at different rates and in some unanticipated ways. Therefore, it is important to consider how employees will react if certain Pillars were transitioned extensively before others have even begun. Since any major inconsistencies across the organization would be uncomfortable or even disruptive, monitoring the rate of adoption of changes and adjusting to allow for some internal harmonizing may be necessary on occasion. In addition, aspects of the forecast preferred environment will evolve in different ways from the original future sketch that was drafted and agreed on, which may change the "destination" or even the direction pursued. So, it is important to select or create metrics that will enable the tracking of the organizational form and elements as they change and allow revised plotting and projecting of where the company is going over time, starting with the prevailing status and associated data points.

As you go through this process, here are some tips to help you start and succeed in the process of transitioning your company to the

Future-of-Work environment and to take full advantage of all the great benefits that are possible.

Tip 1: Get Comfortable

As you get started on the next steps, to set yourself up optimally for success it will help to be mentally-prepared with an open mindset and to consider how to align yourself most comfortably with the prevailing circumstances. Reading this book has hopefully been an important step in that direction. Some (or much) of what you have read may be new to you, so give yourself some time to let the new elements and details register and be absorbed. Other parts are likely familiar, to which additional background and supporting data have added context and explained why we are where we are. The result is hopefully to have facilitated deeper understanding, as well as encouraged more expansive adoption in whatever way is appropriate for your company.

Remember, if you are not truly on board with any particular modifications, you are unlikely to be able to persuade others, and therefore successful implementation is improbable. For areas that you are not totally convinced about or not clear how it might be best to evolve, try exploring more research. You can also ask other people who are interested in making progress in the workplace, and consider their different reactions to the issues in question. It is possible to focus your energies on the areas that you are convinced about and move forward there first. Since the elements are generally interrelated, and the open mindset helps embrace new ideas, recognition of new concepts in related areas is to be expected with greater understanding and practical involvement.

Tip 2: Support Incremental Steps

The range and depth of the changes can feel overwhelming, as can the demands that you may feel confronted by and may possibly be adapting to already. As you know, there is much to be dealt with going forward. The overall recommended and validated approach is to take incremental steps when executing plans, with trials and tweaks along the way. It can then feel much more manageable, and the emphasis can be on all the great progress and benefits to be enjoyed rather than on what is going to hinder your company's transformation. In addition, employees will adapt at their own pace. Legacy habits and practices will change faster and more easily with support and guidance, and then workers' workflow and experiences can also be sustained at reasonable levels throughout the transition.

Tip 3: Dig into the Details

For each element that the transition team deals with, I recommend coming back to this book and thoroughly reviewing all the information in it pertaining to that topic, as well as the studies and research referenced. Where there are aspects that anyone would like more understanding about, additional data and context can help facilitate their choice of appropriate new parameters and smooth adaptation. There are many nuances and details associated with each Pillar and Priority that I have not been able to include in this book. There are simply too many. However, as you and your company embark on this journey to your Future-of-Work environment, for certain elements it will be worthwhile to ensure that you understand and are comfortable with more specifics.

Please also remember to review the lexicon to confirm that you are using the same definitions of the words that I am. In the same vein, consider how to communicate clearly with everyone involved in your company's transformation—including your transition team, executives, managers, and their teams. Shared information is important in creating a common platform of understanding—to generate questions, catalyze dialog, and achieve the buy-in you want.

Tip 4: Check Assumptions

We are all subject to our personal experiences and context in determining how we interpret what we watch, hear, and read. Therefore, during this process it is worthwhile to keep checking the assumptions that might underlie any thought, idea, or premise developed by you and other transition-team members. These are also best communicated with the executives and managers the team coordinates with, and ultimately with the employees themselves, to reduce the chances for misunderstandings or miscommunication.

With analysis of the fundamentals generating the core parameters for the company's future projection, first principles are emphasized, providing neutral ground to discuss and create hypothetical scenarios that may then be tested. It is therefore easier to depersonalize the discussions, creating distance from people's context and assumptions— their historical experiences and associated emotions—in order to prevent these from influencing or affecting the effectiveness of the discussions and outcomes.

Tip 5: Deal with Denial

Many seasoned professionals may have feelings of wistful nostalgia for the patriarchal corporate monoliths of yesteryear. The future workplace looks very different and therefore possibly pretty daunting.

Jobs might have felt more secure until recently, but that hasn't *actually* been the case for a long time already—we are just facing up to the reality now. In addition, I have observed and heard many executives countering, "It's not happening in my _____ (company/sector/ industry)," but it is usually relatively easy to uncover leading signals and indicators by speaking in a little more depth about turnover, engagement, workplace flexibility, and Millennial demands. Perhaps such a response from executives is a hope that the significant transformation, which is intuitively understood, can be delayed, rather than a specific refuting of the inevitability of technology's onward march, or a delusional hope that it may be redirected and accompanying changes disconnected and diverted.

I notice people with blind spots about workplace situations or worker circumstances. I hear denial and have witnessed the associated stress as well. Each company is different, but it is important to take action and make progress, and you are already on the right track or ready to get started. I have found that information is the key to persuading people that change is upon us, and the time for action is now. So, please leverage all the data and documents referenced, which are included for this specific purpose.

"Here's a blank sheet. Let's remake ourselves."

Onward and Upward

To recap, technology is not going to slow down anytime soon, and it is only going to increase, rather than decrease, work options. Furthermore, as noted earlier some estimate that Millennials will reach close to 75 percent of the working population in the United States by 2030. I could say "resistance is futile" and that, worse, it is exhausting. I realize that doesn't help. However, if we remain in "survival" mode, and do not incorporate all the work-related data and insights we now have, we will miss the chance to really flourish and succeed. Employers and workers are facing unprecedented options, as well as the opportunity to make improvements and create working circumstances that are optimized for the company, the business, *and* the workforce.

In moving ahead with such choices, employees will generally be taking on a more diverse set of work tasks and functions and more responsibility for their work focus and format. Flexibility as a mindset, approach, and framework will give your company the agility to adapt to changes in the marketplace and enable mutually beneficial new work arrangements with a strong, value-based and open-minded culture at the core. Significant mutual benefits accrue to employers, employees, and other workers when more flexible ideas, methodologies, and working models are implemented coherently.

You can work proactively to develop your internal talent with a focus on their training and create customized career plans with job rotations that will strengthen their value for mutual benefit. Your business can profit from using independent contractors as their ranks swell. Whatever direction you take, lead with your culture and mindset and focus on the Priorities—engagement, personalization, integration, and choice. If you do so, looking forward and upward, I am confident your workforce will respond positively to the vision, intention, and attention, lifting your organization's potential and raising the probability for greater success in the future.

For me, "progress" is the way to understand, accept, and adapt to what is going on. Leveraging technological advances to run businesses and accomplish tasks more effectively—that's progress. Evaluating talent-related operating practices and exploring ways to improve working circumstances—that's progress. Articulating corporate culture and values to enable workers to align and deepen their connection with their work and employer—that's progress. Loosening work structures to be more responsive to faster marketplace developments and people's lives—that's progress. And nurturing a more "human" work environment that reduces stress and improves health, as well as contributes to better performance—that's progress.

It takes time, effort, energy, and some money to execute a smooth transition to a Future-of-Work environment that will enable your company to be successful going forward. It can be a very bumpy and distracting ride otherwise. It *is* an investment. At the same time, without beating about the bush, I firmly believe it is critical to adapt if your company is to remain competitive and survive. It is progress that you cannot afford not to embrace.

Onwards *and* Upwards.

EPILOGUE

WHAT ELSE IS IMPORTANT?

That is not all! This last section contemplates questions relating to four more important and overarching issues relevant to the overall evolving Future-of-Work ecosystem. My intention in mentioning them is first to highlight other fields and topics that will also benefit from your attention, or at least your consideration that certain changes might affect your company and extended community. Furthermore, considering these additional transitions serves to reinforce the extent and fundamental nature of the overall changes in process.

This section does not seek to provide solutions. Instead, questions that are being raised are shared and some thoughtful answers that are being pondered are floated.

- **Preparing the Workforce:** How well are educational institutions prepared to nurture new generations and support the overall population, allowing them to thrive?

- **Lingering in the Workforce:** Is retirement an out-of-date, and even unhealthy, concept? Would a significant rethink be appropriate?

- **Robots in the Workforce:** How confident are we that millions of jobs being lost to automation *will* be replaced with something else? Isn't it time to consider **basic income** again, properly?

- **The Meaning of Work**: Is the original American Dream still relevant or inclusive enough? Does it need updating?

Preparing the Workforce

Education is an important associated area in transition, impacted both by technology and the evolution of the job market that schools ultimately supply candidates for. In exploring the future needs of education, I spoke with Matthew Breitfelder, the Chief Talent Officer of investment management firm BlackRock, which has more than $5 trillion in assets under management. Breitfelder oversees the hiring, engagement, and retention of thousands of the best investment professionals in the business. He is always in search of excellence and takes a targeted, as well as broad and long-term, approach to talent development and management.

Breitfelder is focused on the critical characteristics of success for talent at BlackRock, both as individuals and in investment-team combinations. He has thoroughly investigated the neuroscience of diversity of thought and utilizes the Science of Inclusion.[109] He is intent on avoiding the pitfalls of hiring like-minded thinkers who are unable to bring a sufficient cross-section of perspectives, whether for generating ideas or evaluating investments. Instead, he promotes the hiring and benefits of a diversity of investors, whose varied strengths are identified and nurtured. He also recognizes the benefit of mindfulness practice for investment professionals, as research indicates it enhances both the ability to focus as well as see patterns.

With thoughtful attention to the Future-of-Work trends, Breitfelder is sensitive to the evolving dynamics of the workforce in relation to the changing skills that are in demand, as well as new approaches to career development. He acknowledges that new emphasis on critical thinking, problem solving, and collaboration will allow people to evaluate and adapt to new and evolving circumstances, even modifying their job descriptions and functions as needed. Breitfelder anticipates these capabilities will only grow in importance and, therefore, a new approach to education overall is needed to prepare Generation Z and beyond for the very different working environments ahead.

Having experienced both Harvard and Oxford tutorial systems himself as a student, Breitfelder considers the applicability of the Socratic method of inquiry and debate that is employed at both educational institutions. This dialectical approach has been used productively for hundreds of years to help develop the type of skills that are increasingly being called upon in the workplace. Breitfelder speculates how it may be effectively applied throughout the American education system, especially in light of new learning technologies such as the Khan Academy.

Breitfelder is also keen for schools to explore the same focus on strengths now being applied within the workforce. He reasons that when students are encouraged to make engagement-driven decisions, compelling outcomes result. Furthermore, Joseph Campbell's "follow your bliss" approach may be effectively harnessed for good subsequent employability, if it is underpinned by pragmatic planning.

These elements are part of Breitfelder's broad-based belief that students will benefit greatly if there is a move to more of a coaching, rather than rote-learning, style of teaching. He suggests this would best be incorporated at the earliest ages, thereby nurturing pupils' involvement in their own education from the beginning. In this way, he believes that students will be better equipped to take greater control of their overall instruction and development. This will in turn prepare them for the increasing self-direction and -management of careers that are becoming the norm.

Breitfelder argues that repetitious teaching practices geared to the lowest common denominator are not going to cultivate a population of flexible and adaptable thinkers that will permit the United States to compete effectively in the global marketplace going forward. With its advancements and personalization capabilities, he envisages technology being efficiently harnessed to provide tools to support this new approach, as well as being customizable for students' different learning strategies and speeds.

Considering the factory-affiliated roots and original purpose of the current school system and methodologies, as mentioned in chapter 1, modification of teaching methodologies to accommodate new workforce needs is imperative. In addition to workers needing different capabilities, their roles are evolving, with new ones emerging and many as yet undefined. Many schools are already reviewing their teaching methods and adapting them for the needs of the future workforce. However, widespread attention is needed to serve the nation's future labor force.

In fact, education is now a continuous theme, as students phase into the realm of work as well as throughout their careers. Technology is also a recurring thread—both driving the learning and providing the means of distribution for the instruction. Training is important for maintaining current knowledge amid marketplace developments, as well as for providing an understanding of new technologies being used or slated for adoption.

How we address education and prepare the next generations for the labor market will be critical for the nation's competitive positioning as we transition to the different future needs of and in the workplace. Back in 2007, the National Academies Press published *Is America Falling Off the Flat Earth?* [110] The chapter "The Competitiveness Equation—The Quality of the Workforce" cites the U.S. Department of Education estimate that "60 percent of the new jobs that will open in the twenty-first century will require skills possessed by only 20 percent of the current workforce." In addition, "Jobs that demand technical training are growing at five times the rate of those requiring nontechnical skills." How are we going to ensure that the current workforce is well-equipped for the new technologies and emerging jobs? How are we modifying the education system to get students ready for their new careers, job profiles, and tasks?

Lingering in the Workforce

Do you really want to retire? If you actually enjoyed your work, had much more flexibility and choice about how, when, and where you work, would you be rushing to retire? Isn't the thought of retirement more about getting away from draining work and rigid hours than about leaving the community of people you work with and the stimulation and sense of accomplishment that some of the projects give you?

In 2002, 20.4 percent of people aged sixty-five to seventy-four in the United States were still working. This number rose to 26.8 percent in 2012 and is projected to reach 31.9 percent in 2022. [111]

At the same time, the average life expectancy of Americans was 73.66 years in 1980, 75.62 years in 1995, and 78.74 in 2012,[112] and it is posited that the first person to live to 150 years old has probably already been born.[113] The later age of those retiring from the workforce in this country and many other countries is mostly a function of people living longer and needing to keep earning money so as not to deplete their savings too soon. At the same time, later retirees are also those who were not thrilled at the idea of "doing nothing" for more than twenty years. Seeing family, playing with grandkids, having time to travel, playing golf, watching TV, and sitting on the front porch observing the world go by are all wonderful pastimes—but not necessarily for two decades or more!

Whatever your retirement means, at whatever age, an important consideration is to engage your brain in ways that actively maintain your synapse connections and make new neurons. There is now compelling new evidence about the brain's plasticity and how mental activity is important in preventing cognitive decline.[114] There is also data that indicates the same for physical activity, insofar as maintaining an active life helps reduce cognitive decline and dementia.[115]

At the same time, the trade-offs that made retirement the long-desired escape from work are being revised. Technology's advances and Future-of-Work adaptations are increasingly enabling working formats that allow for visits to grandkids, rounds of golf, *and* a number of office hours and/or project work per week to be achieved. Therefore, rather than longing to distance yourself from work as soon as possible, a positive approach to your more mature years might be to stay involved in the workforce. A semi-retirement plan can keep your brain in a healthy state, as well as your bank balance.

More flexible, phased retirement arrangements are actively promoted in the U.K.[116] as well as the U.S.,[117] acknowledging the aging workforce. The proposition is to allow the employer to value and share the expertise and experience of the senior worker with other employees, at a reduced cost. Meanwhile, older employees remain actively engaged in work, with reduced hours and more flexible schedules. They feel valued, they are able to participate in a greater variety of noncorporate activities, and they are more likely to stay healthy when mentally and physically engaged in a broad range of corporate and noncorporate activities.

Certain changes will encourage or are necessary to allow for these phased-retirement and reduced-working arrangements. Some corporate pension plans are not flexible enough to permit ongoing contributions in scenarios such as reduced hours. In addition, non-corporate retirement-savings plans are important to help the increasing numbers of senior workers who are moving to consulting and freelance arrangements. Overall, don't you think our labor force will benefit from continuing to include older workers, enriched by the diversity of perspectives and experiences? Does your company already have a way to cater to new or reduced schedules for older members of your workforce? How can your company pair more seasoned workers with younger ones to share expertise and experience?

Robots in the Workforce

In 2013, it was predicted that 47 percent of U.S. jobs were at "high risk" of being automated away by 2034.[118] That would obviously mean millions of people out of work. The image seems dramatic, alarming, and even far-fetched—armies of robots sitting in the seats of displaced workers. However, the reality is more subtle and impactful. For example, at the beginning of 2017, a "traditional" company such as Walmart employed 1.5 million people in the United

States (and 2.3 million people worldwide), and another, General Motors, employed 215,000 worldwide. Meanwhile, new "digital-economy" companies, benefiting from integrated technology efficiencies, had far fewer: Facebook had fewer than 16,000 employees and Twitter fewer than 4,000. Amazon—which topped Walmart in 2015 to become America's largest retailer—online or off—had just over 240,000. Businesses are being built differently, leveraging technology platforms and applications. Meanwhile, driverless trucks are already poised to replace a substantial portion of the estimated 3.5 million truckers in the United States.[119]

"What if we don't change at all... and something magical just happens?"

Even if the number of jobs lost and not replaced by other roles is far fewer than predicted—perhaps only 20 or 25 percent—that still amounts to millions of people. What are the potential solutions? What about shorter workweeks, with the aggregate pool of working hours allocated among available workers to share the fewer hours of "human work"? What about reskilling? Helping workers retrain and adapt to new job options will certainly occur widely going forward, as will continuing education related to technology developments. Millions will likely undergo training several times over the course of their multiple careers. However, it seems unlikely that any of these solutions—or all of them together—will be sufficient.

Basic income is a broad-based possible solution coming at the problem from a different angle. Basic income is "a periodic cash payment unconditionally delivered to all on an individual basis, without means test or work requirement."[120] It is not a new idea. It has appealed to numerous economists and both sides of the political aisle since Sir Thomas More dreamt of it in *Utopia* in 1516.[121] President Nixon proposed it in 1969 when the President's Commission on Income Maintenance Programs issued *Poverty Amid Plenty: The American Paradox*, which even included suggested dollar amounts that would be paid to each adult and child per year. The proposal got through the House with a majority in April 1970 but then stalled in the Senate. Now that automation is changing the job market significantly, there is more discussion about basic income and other possible options to fund the support of a large structurally "disemployed" population. How are we going to ensure the labor force has the skills to adapt to the new jobs? How are we going to support those whose jobs have been eliminated permanently by digital transformation? What are the viable alternatives to basic income?

The Meaning of Progress

We have measured our progress by means of our economic activity, mostly focused on our production output, thanks to the invaluable work of the "father of economics," Adam Smith, in his 1776 tome *The Wealth of Nations*. This was followed up in 1937 by Simon Kuznets, an economist at the National Bureau of Economic Research, who devised the original formulation of gross domestic product (GDP). GDP is the monetary value of all the finished goods and services produced within a country's borders in a specific time period. It measures national economic activity and has also long been equated with a country's standard of living.

However, GDP neither captures the quality of our lives nor acknowledges the precious resources of the planet that we have been consuming with abandon for centuries. In the original American Dream, we captured the measure of the opportunity we needed and desired at the time. However, our current circumstances are very different. Now, "work" has new meaning and purpose for many people. Now, the global population is more than seven billion, and the reduced resources of our planet are limited and more valuable. Now, experiences are also important life objectives, shifting the emphasis from accumulation of assets. Now, quality of life is rising as a measure of success and achievement.

What are we really striving for now? Are we not seeking to prosper as well? What does progress really mean to each one of us? Should new elements not also be represented in the American Dream?

FUTURE OF WORK
LEXICON

WORDS AND MEANINGS

alternative-employment arrangements. As defined by the Bureau
of Labor Statistics in 2005 encompasses: Independent contractors—
workers who were identified as independent contractors, independent
consultants, or freelance workers; On-call workers—workers who
are called to work only as needed; temporary-help-agency workers—
workers who were paid by a temporary-help agency, whether or
not their job was temporary; workers provided by contract firms,
employed by a company that provides them or their services to others
under contract, usually assigned to one customer.

artificial intelligence. Computer capability to perform operations
that are similar to the learning and decision-making of humans.

big data. Any voluminous amount of data—ranging from structured to unstructured—that can be mined for information and insights.

career-experience management. Acknowledgement and management of the entire work experience, comprising daily tasks and environment, as well as all elements of the long-term planning, guiding, and supporting of the series of positions held by the person.

conscious capitalism. A way of thinking about capitalism and business that better reflects the current state of the world and the potential of business to make a positive impact on it.

chronologically-formatted resume. See **resume.**

contingent workers. Those who do not have an implicit or explicit contract for ongoing employment. These include wage and salary workers who expect their jobs to last for one more year or less and who had worked at their jobs for one year or less, and self-employed and independent contractors who expect their employment to last for one more year or less, and they had been self-employed or independent contractors for one year or less. As defined by the Bureau of Labor Statistics in 2005.

digital transformation. The fundamental change caused by the embedded integration of technology into the operating processes and practices of a business, allowing for new types of innovation and models rather than just incrementally improving traditional practices.

diversified or portfolio career. New career models that include two or more concurrent positions or projects, bringing in multiple revenue streams, and possibly including more than one use of the person's skills or use in more than one sector.

efficiency. Historically associated with accomplishing a task with the minimum of expenditure of time and effort, the meaning is potentially evolving to be more focused on the optimal way to accomplish a task, taking into account employee-engagement benefits and other talent-related consequences, not just least input.

"Time for Lesson 1 in our new language."

framework. A more flexible, hierarchically-flatter, umbrella-type organization-design concept which contrasts to a traditional fixed multi-level hierarchical structure.

functionally-formatted resume. See **resume.**

Future of Work. An umbrella term that encompasses the multitude of changes in transition in the workplace and with the workforce, including but not limited to workplace flexibility, purpose-driven culture, employee-engagement issues, flatter hierarchy, and diversified and latticed careers.

future sketch. This is the Future-of-Work projection specific to your company. You can give it a different name, however, the "sketch" concept is useful as it implies a pencil drawing that is clear but can be modified and allow for evolution over time as necessary.

gig economy. A labor market where short-term engagements—notably freelance or independent contract work—are common, rather than long-term full-time jobs.

hackathon. An event that brings people of diverse disciplines together to solve problems. Originating from computer programming-related occasions.

integration. In this book, this term generally refers to the embedded incorporation of technology into a company's fundamental business operations, as well as the pervasive assimilation of particular values, mindsets, policies, and practices throughout an organization and its environment.

Internet of Things. The interrelated connectivity of billions of computers and other digital devices and elements that are able to share data over the network seamlessly and without human intervention.

knowledge worker. A knowledge worker is anyone who works for a living at the tasks of developing or using knowledge, such as lawyers, scientists, information technologists, and management consultants.

latticed career. A career with non-linear progression, including lateral and or diagonal subsequent positions.

mentoring culture. A company with a culture that promotes their employees nurturing, managing, and supporting each other's learning and development.

mindset. The established set of attitudes held by someone.

organization design. Development of the plan and process for how a corporation is to be organized and run.

personalization. In this book, personalization refers specifically to the individually-focused customization of talent-related elements.

personal business plan. An approach for developing an employee's career plan, considering it analogous to an individual independent enterprise. For example, the income from a person's future jobs and project fees would be equivalent to their personal business's revenue streams.

productivity. An evaluation of production efficiency, historically measuring output per unit of input that has typically been labor and/ or capital.

resume. A short summary of a person's education, professional experience, and qualifications. *Chronological format:* Experiences are described in reverse chronological order, starting with the current or most recent position listed first. *Functional format:* The summary is organized around the skills of the person rather than linear sequence of positions held, with competency-related achievements and roles highlighted.

shadow IT. The use by an employee of a technology that has not been approved by the company for corporate use.

social responsibility. The concept of promoting businesses to incorporate societal benefits together with profit objectives.

talent agenda. The worker-related elements, initiatives and policies that govern how an organization manages and focuses upon its workforce.

well-being. The state of being healthy, happy, and prosperous.

working profile. The outline of a person's combination of work tasks, style, model (including work location(s)), and schedule.

workplace flexibility. Any working profile for which the schedule is not 9 o'clock a.m. to 5 o'clock p.m., five days a week—including a compressed work week, partially or wholly working remotely, or a five-day workweek with flexible hours.

ENDNOTES

1   "U.S. Employee Engagement," Gallup, (2015).

2   "State of the American Workplace," Gallup, (2013).

3   "The State of American Vacation: How vacation became a casualty of our work culture," *Project: Time Off* (2016): http://www.projecttimeoff.com/research/state-american-vacation-2016.

4   Kenneth Matos and Ellen Galinsky, "2014 National Study of Employers," *Families and Work.Org* (2014): http://familiesandwork.org/downloads/2014NationalStudyOfEmployers.pdf.

5   Labor Department, (August 2016).

6   "State of the Industry: Employee Wellbeing, Culture and Engagement in 2017," VirginPulse.

7   Christian Fuchs, *Reading Marx in the Information Age* (London: Routledge, 2015), 132.

8   Cecil Bohanon, "Economic Recovery: Lessons from the Post-World War II Period," Mercatus on Policy (2010): https://www.mercatus.org/system/files/PostWWII_Recovery_Bohanon_MOP112-(1)-copy.pdf.

9   "Historical Census of Housing Tables" *The United States Census Bureau* (2012): https://www.census.gov/hhes/www/housing/census/historic/values.html.

10   "Current Population Reports. Consumer Income," *U.S. Department of Commerce* (1961): http://www2.census.gov/prod2/popscan/p60-035.pdf.

11   "Changes in men's and women's labor force participation rates," U.S. Bureau of Labor Statistics,(January 10, 2007), https://www.bls.gov/opub/ted/2007/

jan/wk2/art03.htm.

12   U.S. Bureau of Labor Statistics.

13   Pew Research Center.

14   "Prussian Education System," World Heritage Encyclopedia, http://www.
     worldheritage.org/article/WHEBN0004206694/Prussian%20education%20
     system.

15   Gordon E. Moore. "Cramming more components onto integrated
     circuits," *Electronics Magazine* 38, no.8 (1965): https://drive.google.com/
     file/d/0By83v5TWkGjvQkpBcXJKT1I1TTA/view.

16   Klaus Schwab, "The Fourth Industrial Revolution: what it means and how
     to respond," *World Economic Forum Annual Meeting* (2016): eforum.org/
     agenda/2016/01/the-fourth-industrial-revolution-what-it-means-and-how-
     to-respond/.

17   John Calvin, *Institutes of the Christian Religion* (1536).

18   "How Millennials Want to Work and Live," *Gallup Report* (May 2016).

19   "State of the Industry: Employee Wellbeing, Culture and Engagement in
     2017," VirginPulse.

20   Sophie Wade, "Productivity And Performance With A Distributed
     Workforce: Control, Choice, And Communication," *Digitalist Magazine*
     (2016): http://www.digitalistmag.com/future-of-work/2016/08/24/
     productivity-performance-with-distributed-workforce-04410454.

21   Gartner Report, (November 2015).

22   "Cisco Global Cloud Index: Forecast and Methodology, 2015-2020," *Cisco
     Public* (2016): http://www.cisco.com/c/dam/en/us/solutions/collateral/
     service-provider/global-cloud-index-gci/white-paper-c11-738085.pdf.

23   Pew Research Center survey, (June-July 2015).

24   Sophie Wade, "Productivity And Performance With A Distributed
     Workforce: Control, Choice, And Communication."

25   "IDC FutureScape: Worldwide IT Industry 2017 Predictions,"
     IDC.com, (2016): abstract at https://www.idc.com/getdoc.
     jsp?containerId=US41883016.

26   U.S. Census Bureau, "Analysis of 2005-2014 American
     Community Survey," *GlobalWorkplaceAnalytics.com* (2016): http://
     globalworkplaceanalytics.com/telecommuting-statistics.

27   Ibid.

28   "Freelancing in America. A National Survey of the New Workforce, an
     independent survey," *Freelancers Union and Elance-oDesk* (September,
     2014): https://fu-web-storage-prod.s3.amazonaws.com/content/
     filer_public/7c/45/7c457488-0740-4bc4-ae45-0aa60daac531/

freelancinginamerica_report.pdf.

29   "Set Them Free: How Alternative Work Styles Can be a Good Fit," *Herman Miller, Inc.* (2007): http://www.hermanmiller.com/research/research-summaries/set-them-free-how-alternative-work-styles-can-be-a-good-fit.html.

30   Eric Richert and David Rush, "The new work environment: A systems approach to infrastructure design," *Sun Microsystems*, October 14, 2005, http://www.sun.com/service/openwork/artic.les/journal_corp_real_estate.pdf.

31   Naufal Khan, Jason Reynolds, and Christoph Schrey,"Partnering to shape the future—IT's new imperative," *McKinsey & Company* (2016): http://www.mckinsey.com/business-functions/digital-mckinsey/our-insights/partnering-to-shape-the-future-its-new-imperative.

32   Maura Hudson, "Facility Management Trend Report. Emerging Opportunities for Industry Leaders," *IFMA in conjunction with CBRE* (2014): http://www.cbre.us/services/research/AssetLibrary/2014%20IFMA%20CBRE%20Trend%20Report.pdf.

33   "Thriving in the Digital Economy: The Innovative Finance Function," *CFO Research in collaboration with SAP* (2015): http://www.sap.com/docs/download/2015/11/50209790-4a7c-0010-82c7-eda71af511fa.pdf.

34   Joshua Tauberer, "How to run a successful hackathon," *Hackathon Guide* (2015): https://hackathon.guide/.

35   "Generations at Work," *Herman Miller, Inc.* (2010): http://www.hermanmiller.com/research/research-summaries/generations-at-work.html.

36   Pip Coburn, Coburn Ventures, (November 2015).

37   Kyle S. Smith, Arti Virkud, Karl Deisseroth, and Ann M. Greybiel, "Reversible online control of habitual behavior by optogenetic perturbation of medial prefrontal cortex," *Proceedings of the National Academy of Sciences* 109, no. 46, 2012.

38   "Millennials at work. Reshaping the workplace," Pwc.com (2011): https://www.pwc.com/gx/en/managing-tomorrows-people/future-of-work/assets/reshaping-the-workplace.pdf.

39   2015 Census.

40   "How Millennials Want to Work and Live," *Gallup Report*, (May 2016).

41   Pew Research Center, (2016).

42   "Employee Satisfaction vs. Employee Engagement: Are They the Same Thing?" ADP Research Institute, (2012).

43   John Calvin, *Institutes of the Christian Religion* (1536).

44   *Oxford English Dictionary,* s.v. "compensation."

45   "How Millennials Want to Work and Live," *Gallup Report,* (May 2016).

46   Aaron Hurst and Anna Tavis, "2015 Workforce Purpose Index. Work orientations of the U.S. workforce and associated predictive indicators of performance and wellbeing," *Imperative and New York University* (2015): https://cdn.imperative.com/media/public/Purpose_Index_2015.

47   David Batman and Olivia Sackett, "Clocking On and Checking Out. Why Your Employees May Not Be Working at Optimal Levels and What You Can Do about It," *GCC Insights. Get the World Moving* (2016): http://info. gettheworldmoving.com/rs/018-WUL-420/images/presenteeism-whitepaper. pdf.

48   Ibid.

49   Amy Kristof-Brown, Ryan Zimmerman, and Erin Johnson, "Consequences of Individuals' Fit at Work: A Meta-Analysis of Person-Job, Person-Organization, Person-Group, and Person-Supervisor Fit," *Personnel Psychology* (2005): abstract at http://onlinelibrary.wiley.com/doi/10.1111/ j.1744-6570.2005.00672.x/abstract.

50   Susan Sorenson, "How Employees' Strengths Make Your Company Stronger," *Gallup Report* (2014): http://www.gallup.com/ businessjournal/167462/employees-strengths-company-stronger.aspx.

51   Jim Asplund and Nikki Blacksmith, "Stengthening Your Company's Performance," Gallup, (March 1, 2011), http://www.gallup.com/ businessjournal/146351/strengthening-company-performance.aspx.

52   İzlem Gözükara· and Omer Faruk Şimşek, "Linking Transformational Leadership to Work Engagement and the Mediator Effect of Job Autonomy: A Study in a Turkish Private Non-Profit University," *Procedia* 195 (2015): 963-971 http://www.sciencedirect.com/science/article/pii/ S1877042815037532.

53   Raghuram Rajan and Julie Wulf, "The Flattening Firm: Evidence from Panel Data on the Changing Nature of Corporate Hierarchies," *National Bureau of Economic Research Working Paper Series, Working Paper #9633,* (April 2003): http://www.nber.org/papers/w9633 (accessed March 2, 2009).

54   "Better Smarter Faster. Accelerating innovation across the enterprise," *Jama Software White Paper* (2013): http://www.jamasoftware.com/wp-content/ uploads/documents/jama-better-smarter-faster-accelerating-innovation-across-the%E2%80%93enterprise.pdf.

55   Peter F. Drucker, *Management Challenges for the 21ˢᵗ Century* (New York: Harper Business, 2001).

56   Peter F. Drucker, *The Practice of Management* (New York: Harper Business, 2006).

57   "The State of American Vacation: How vacation became a casualty of our

work culture," Project: Time Off (2016): http://www.projecttimeoff.com/research/state-american-vacation-2016.

58   "State of the American Workplace: Employee Engagement Insights for U.S. Business Leaders," *Gallup* (2013): http://employeeengagement.com/wp-content/uploads/2013/06/Gallup-2013-State-of-the-American-Workplace-Report.pdf.

59   U.S. Labor Department.

60   "The Malcolm Baldridge Criteria for Performance Excellence," (2005).

61   Lindsay Gellman and Justin Baer, "Goldman Sachs to Stop Rating Employees with Numbers, *The Wall Street Journal* (May 2016): http://www.marketwatch.com/story/goldman-sachs-dumps-employee-ranking-system-2016-05-26-101033047.

62   Marcus Buckingham and Ashley Goodall, "Reinventing Performance Management," *Harvard Business Review* (April 2015): https://hbr.org/2015/04/reinventing-performance-management.

63   "Better Smarter Faster. Accelerating innovation across the enterprise," *Jama Software White Paper* (2013): http://www.jamasoftware.com/wp-content/uploads/documents/jama-better-smarter-faster-accelerating-innovation-across-the%E2%80%93enterprise.pdf.

64   Jay Van Bavel and Dominic Packer, "The Problem with Rewarding Individual Performers," *Harvard Business Review* (December 2016): https://hbr.org/2016/12/the-problem-with-rewarding-individual-performers.

65   Amy Kristof-Brown, Ryan Zimmerman, and Erin Johnson, "Consequences of Individuals' Fit at Work: A Meta-Analysis of Person-Job, Person-Organization, Person-Group, and Person-Supervisor Fit," *Personnel Psychology* (2005): abstract at http://onlinelibrary.wiley.com/doi/10.1111/j.1744-6570.2005.00672.x/abstract.

66   2105 Workforce Purpose Index, Imperative and NYU.

67   "Global Workforce Happiness Index," Universum, (2015), http://universumglobal.com/happinessindex/.

68   Brian Gifford, "Linking Workforce Health to Business Performance Metrics: Strategies, Challenges and Opportunities," *Integrated Benefits Institute* (September 2015): https://ibiweb.org/?ACT=65&id=nNXqF1ZCrmSMdVQt347T7CLC_og7FCWMqISJKp2Lni1Ooi0rCbTzoT-9JtA55Cdw0Wj-f0R9KMEWEqZ57_boouQ5-N9NyZyucyL0_n-Nl0ysPDgDeiwDi6TPBnU0ObI6.

69   "Program Measurement and Evaluation Guide. Core Metrics for Employee Health Management," *Health Enhancement Research Organization and Population Health Alliance* (2015): https://www.shrm.org/ResourcesAndTools/hr-topics/benefits/Documents/HERO-PHA-Metrics-

Guide-FINAL.pdf.

70   Framingham Heart Study, (2010), www.framinghamheartstudy.org/index. php.

71   Stevan Hobfoll and Arie Shirom, "Conservation of of resources theory: Applications to stress and management in the workplace," *Public Policy and Administration* 87, (January 2001).

72   "The Business of Healthy Employees. A Survey of Workplace Health Priorities," *Workforce and Virgin Pulse* (2016): http://connect. virginpulse.com/files/VP_Business_of_Healthy_Employees_FINALcor. pdf?submissionGuid=fcb0b53b-9529-4049-8d68-c29a9c27e666.

73   "State of the Industry: Employee Wellbeing, Culture and Engagement in 2017," VirginPulse.

74   "Flexible working and work-life balance," *ACAS* (2015): http://www.acas. org.uk/media/pdf/j/m/Flexible-working-and-work-life-balance.pdf.

75   Richard Foster and Sarah Kaplan, *Creative Destruction* (Crown Business, 2001).

76   "The Ecosystem Equation: Collaboration in the Connected Economy," *Harvard Business Review Analytic Services Report* (2016): https://hbr.org/ resources/pdfs/comm/ibm/19829_HBR_Report_IBM_June2016.pdf.

77   Nick Bloom, Tobias Krestchmer, and John Van Reenen, "Work-Life Balance, Management Practices and Productivity," (April 2006).

78   "The right to request flexible working," ACAS, http://www.acas.org.uk/ index.aspx?articleid=1616.

79   International Labour Organization, www.ilo.org.

80   "Presidential Memorandum -- Enhancing Workplace Flexibilities and Work-Life Program," (June 2014): https://obamawhitehouse.archives. gov/the-press-office/2014/06/23/presidential-memorandum-enhancing-workplace-flexibilities-and-work-life-.

81   Sophie Wade, "The Future of Work: The Co-Evolution of Humans and Robots OR I Heart My Robo-Assistant," *The Huffington Post* (2016): http://www. huffingtonpost.com/sophie-wade/the-future-of-work-the-co_b_9769278.html.

82   "Maslow's Humanistic Theory of Personality," *Boundless.com* (2016): https:// www.boundless.com/psychology/textbooks/boundless-psychology-textbook/ personality-16/humanistic-perspectives-on-personality-78/maslow-s-humanistic-theory-of-personality-307-12842/.

83   Sophie Wade, "The Future of Work: The Co-Evolution of Humans and Robots OR I Heart My Robo-Assistant."

84   Katherine W. Phillips, "How Diversity Makes Us Smarter," *Scientific American* (2014): https://www.scientificamerican.com/article/how-diversity-

makes-us-smarter/.

85   Christine Cox, et. al, "The Science of Inclusion," *NeuroLeadership Journal.*

86   "Office Design Case Study: How Cisco Designed the Collaborative Connected Workplace Environment," Cisco, http://www.cisco.com/c/en/us/about/cisco-on-cisco/collaboration/connected-workplace-web.html.

87   "Set Them Free: How Alternative Work Styles Can be a Good Fit," *Herman Miller, Inc.* (2007): http://www.hermanmiller.com/research/research-summaries/set-them-free-how-alternative-work-styles-can-be-a-good-fit.html.

88   Philip Ross, "Activity Based Working. The Hybrid Organisation: Buildings," *Microsoft.com/UK* (2008): https://www.generation-e.com.au/attachments/article/188/activity-based-working.pdf.

89   Jay Van Bavel and Dominic Packer, "The Problem with Rewarding Individual Performers," *Harvard Business Review* (December 2016): https://hbr.org/2016/12/the-problem-with-rewarding-individual-performers.

90   "The Private to Open Spectrum," *Herman Miller, Inc.* (2013): http://www.hermanmiller.com/content/dam/hermanmiller/documents/research_summaries/wp_Private_to_Open.pdf.

91   "The Privacy Crisis. Taking a toll on employee engagement," *Steelcase* (2014): https://www.steelcase.com/content/uploads/2014/11/360Magazine-Issue68.pdf.

92   "Home Sweet Office: Comfort in the Workplace." *Herman Miller, Inc.* (2015): http://www.hermanmiller.com/content/dam/hermanmiller/documents/research_summaries/wp_Comfort_in_the_Workplace.pdf.

93   "The Ecosystem Equation: Collaboration in the Connected Economy," *Harvard Business Review* (2016): https://hbr.org/resources/pdfs/comm/ibm/19829_HBR_Report_IBM_June2016.pdf.

94   Ibid.

95   Christopher J. Dwyer, "The State of Contingent Workforce Management 2016-17," *Ardent Partners* (2016): http://resources.fieldglass.com/rs/655-SDM-567/images/Ardent_Partners_The_State_of_CWM_2015_Fieldglass.pdf?mkt_tok=3RkMMJWWfF9wsRoivKzLZKXonjHpfsX67%2BQqWq%2B1lMI/0ER3fOvrPUfGjI4ES8RnI%2BSLDwEYGJlv6SgFTLXAMbNk17gIXRY%3D.

96   "Freelancing in America: 2016," *Freelancers Union and UpWork* (2016): http://www.harrywalker.com/media/1400666/rinne_april-freelancinginamerica2016report.pdf.

97   Christopher J. Dwyer, "The State of Contingent Workforce Management 2016-17."

98   Ibid.

99 U.S. Bureau of Labor Statistics.

100 Seth D. Harris and Alan B. Krueger, "A Proposal for Modernizing Labor Law for Twenty-First Century Work: The 'Independent Worker,'" *The Hamilton Project* (2015): http://www.hamiltonproject.org/assets/files/ modernizing_labor_laws_for_twenty_first_century_work_krueger_harris. pdf.

101 Ibid.

102 Gallup Strengths Center, https://www.gallupstrengthscenter.com/.

103 Susan Sorenson, "How Employees' Strengths Make Your Company Stronger,"., *Gallup Report* (2014): http://www.gallup.com/ businessjournal/167462/employees-strengths-company-stronger.aspx.

104 Colin Beavan, pers. comm.

105 Douglas Elmendorf, Gregory Mankiw, and Lawrence H. Summers, eds. *Brookings Papers on Economic Activity: Spring 2008* (Washington: Brookings Institution Press, 2008).

106 Cathy Benko and Warren McFarlan, "Managing a growth culture: how CEOs can initiate and monitor a successful growth-project culture," *Strategy & Leadership* 32 no. 1 (2004) 34-42. doi: http://dx.doi. org/10.1108/10878570410511408.

107 Patheer, Patheer.com.

108 Alice Truong, "'You're a real sweetheart': The surprisingly human ways people respond to an AI assistant," Quartz, (February 29, 2016), https:// qz.com/626652/youre-a-real-sweetheart-the-surprisingly-human-ways- people-respond-to-an-ai-assistant/.

109 Christine Cox, et. al, "The Science of Inclusion," *NeuroLeadership Journal*.

110 *Is America Falling Off the Flat Earth?,* National Academies of Science and Engineering and the Institute of Medicine, (2007).

111 U.S. Bureau of Labor Statistics.

112 World Bank.

113 Aubrey de Grey, researcher at Cambridge University.

114 Dr. Michael Merzenich, professor emeritus at the University of California.

115 Sarah J. Blondell, Rachel Hammersley-Mather, and J. Lennert Veerman, "Does physical activity prevent cognitive decline and dementia?: A systematic review and meta-analysis of longitudinal studies" BMC Public Health (2014): https://bmcpublichealth.biomedcentral.com/ articles/10.1186/1471-2458-14-510.

116 Dr. Emma Parry, "Managing an aging workforce. The role of total reward." Chartered Institute of Personnel and Development (2006).

117 Chantel Sheaks, "Legal and Research Summary Sheet: Phased Retirement," *Georgetown University Law Center* (2010): http://workplaceflexibility2010. org/images/uploads/PhasedRetirement08-07.pdf.

118 Carl Benedikt Frey and Michael A. Osborne, The Future of Employment: How Susceptible Are Jobs to Computerisation?" *University of Oxford* (2013): http://www.oxfordmartin.ox.ac.uk/downloads/academic/The_Future_of_ Employment.pdf.

119 James Donley, "Automation Will Change the Trucking Industry Forever," *Acies Group* (2016): http://aciesgroup.com/wp-content/uploads/2017/01/ Automation-Will-Change-The-Trucking-Industry-Forever.pdf.

120 "About Basic Income," *Basic Income Earth Network*, http://basicincome.org/ basic-income/.

121 Rutger Bregman, "Why We Should Give Free Money to Everyone," *The Correspondent* (2014): https://thecorrespondent.com/541/why-we-should- give-free-money-to-everyone/20798745-cb9fbb39.

SERVICES

NEXT STEPS FOR EMBRACING PROGRESS

I f you would like some help taking the next steps to inform and transform your organization for the Future of Work, visit SophieWade.com to find out how to engage Sophie to speak at or consult to your company.

CONSULTING

Sophie can bring her deep knowledge and experience to assist your organization in creating an appropriate future sketch of your desired Future-of-Work environment. She can help you evaluate your company's current status, looking at different areas and working with you to consider relevant prioritization for adaptation. Sophie utilizes her expertise to support the development and implementation of strategic transition plans including trials and roll-out. Sophie will enable your company to make the transformation to your desired new working environment with the least disruption possible.

SPEAKING

Sophie speaks regularly about Future-of-Work topics including employee engagement and retention, talent management, workplace flexibility, intergenerational challenges, career experience management, and latticed and diversified careers. She talks to large and small internal and external corporate and general audiences in addition to engaging in workshop sessions, depending on the focus, intention, and desired outcomes.